"Very few people have enjoyed high positions in different realms, excelled in them, and then found greater liberty and independence in their second acts. In his first act, Balji's intellect, wit and bottomless barrel of pithy headlines made him a public figure as a journalist and editor, one that people might profess to know through his writing. Woon Tai Ho's candid and personal writing lifts the veil behind that public persona, gifting us an insight into significant life events, a peek into his intellectual foundation and at the evolution of his character and outlook. Most striking are the moments of reflection, at times vulnerable, where the conversations between Balji and the author veer into what feels like previously unexplored territory. This feels like Balji beyond the headlines, through the eyes of a close friend and those of his loved ones."

Sumana Rajarethnam
Global Head of Strategy and Outreach,
Trust and Safety, Kuaishou

"[A] timely book ... expect to understand a little bit more of what makes a successful editor – one who is able to navigate both political and financial pressures – tick ... In shaping a newspaper, Balji also shaped a part of Singapore society and culture."

Professor Ang Peng Hwa
Wee Kim Wee School of Communication
and Information, NTU

"Written by an impassioned documentary veteran, this book warms the heart and soul. Vivid anecdotes from the doyen of the Singapore print media abound, and his everyday life experiences shine a guiding light for the younger generation during a pandemic."

Shu Qi
Founder, Doyenne Singapore

"Tai Ho's classic writing style brings to life the real person behind the personality we all know as PN Balji: a veteran journalist and astute observer of the world around us. ... The stories here revolve around his role as husband, father and now grandfather, and it is being told against the backdrop of the man and his daily obsession with everything about modern-day Singapore. Truly admirable piece of work; the man and the book!"

Azman Jaafar
Managing Partner, RHTLaw Asia LLP

"Tai Ho has captured the man, his family and his journey very well indeed; but this is an unfinished story. Given the rapidly changing regional dynamics, there certainly is a place for a Balji with his Naval Base embedded DNA and, more so, for countless young Singaporeans like Balji's grandson (who has already published a book) to also carry their unique torches to ensure Singapore emerges a thriving and vibrant marketplace of competing ideas and challenging opinions."

Verghese Mathews
Veteran diplomat

"Those with an interest in Singapore's socio-political scene will know Balji from his incisive commentaries and role in creating two newspapers ... Tai Ho takes us a step further by showcasing Balji the person and describing the many activities Balji took up after 'retiring' from *TODAY* in 2003. I highly recommend this book to those who want to know more about a giant in the local media scene and are thinking about a second life post-retirement."

Kevin Lim
Financial journalist/editor

"The golden rule in journalism is to 'show, don't tell'. PN Balji has embodied that maxim throughout his distinguished career, showing generations of Singaporeans the importance and value of independent journalism in a free-thinking, fair-minded society. Balji's passion for his chosen profession as an editor and writer shows in the bravery, honesty, and incisiveness of his remarkable and ongoing work. Balji's example, his caring insight and sage advice continue to be taken to heart by the oldest and youngest among us, from journalists in this profession to citizens in this world."

Tom Benner
Award-winning journalist; writer, editor, instructor

"In the early years of RICE Media, Balji was instrumental in giving us the determination to create an independent and alternative publication that centres around RICE's unique brand of investigative journalism. ... The tireless support of veteran journalists such as Balji is essential to the growth of publications such as ours today, without which, the vibrancy of Singapore's journalism space would be of little guarantee. This book underlines that spirit of independence we have grown to associate with Balji."

Mark Tan
Founder & CEO, Editor-in-Chief, RICE Media

"Balji is one of the most insightful commentators on the societal and political scene in Singapore and beyond. This book offers a rare opportunity to find out more about the true story of the person behind those insights as well as the family and community that come through in every conversation as being so important to him."

Richard Hartung
Former banker

"Woon Tai Ho, novelist, biographer, Channel NewsAsia founder and, most recently, the author of a biography on artist Lim Tze Peng, is unafraid to ask hard questions of Balji to winkle out the man behind the more commonly known media commentator. ... Balji has new, urgent insights into Singapore politics, living in the republic, and life itself, that contemporary readers can gain much benefit from. ... [This book] is also timely because of the very personal interplay between author and subject that is revelatory about issues today of identity and mortality.

The great communicator, as his admiring former colleagues call him, shows why he has earned a permanent place in Singapore's own narrative, with a story in the capable hands of Woon that is disarmingly open, knowledgeable, entertaining, and wise indeed, for our troubled times."

Linda Collins
author of *Loss Adjustment* (Ethos Books, 2019)

"PN Balji has had a ringside seat to the drama of Singapore's national story. His reflections, sensitively chronicled and interpreted by Woon Tai Ho, should be used by Singaporeans to frame the big questions that we face going forward – and our answers to those questions, inevitably disparate as these will be. Particularly enjoyable are Balji's thoughts on the relevance of retirement and Singapore's growing desire for political pluralism as a corrective to elite complacency, authoritarianism and group-think."

Leon Perera
MP for Aljunied GRC

TRANSITION
The Story of PN Balji

Woon Tai Ho

Marshall Cavendish
Editions

Published in 2022 by Marshall Cavendish Editions
An imprint of Marshall Cavendish International

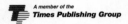

A member of the
Times Publishing Group

Other Marshall Cavendish Offices:
Marshall Cavendish Corporation, 800 Westchester Ave, Suite N-641, Rye Brook, NY 10573, USA • Marshall Cavendish International (Thailand) Co Ltd, 253 Asoke, 16th Floor, Sukhumvit 21 Road, Klongtoey Nua, Wattana, Bangkok 10110, Thailand • Marshall Cavendish (Malaysia) Sdn Bhd, Times Subang, Lot 46, Subang Hi-Tech Industrial Park, Batu Tiga, 40000 Shah Alam, Selangor Darul Ehsan, Malaysia

National Library Board, Singapore Cataloguing-in-Publication Data

Name(s): Woon, Tai Ho, 1958-
Title: Transition : the story of PN Balji / Woon Tai Ho.
Description: Singapore : Marshall Cavendish Editions, 2022.
Identifier(s): ISBN 978-981-5044-01-0 (paperback)
Subject(s): LCSH: P. N., Balji | Journalists--Singapore--Biography. |
   Reporters and reporting--Singapore. | Journalism--Singapore.
Classification: DDC 079.5957--dc23

Printed in Singapore

In loving memory of my parents

CONTENTS

CONTENTS

Foreword

Journalists are, in essence, storytellers. Some stick to facts. Others venture into opinions. Ultimately, they all want to tell interesting stories. Here is a story of one storyteller by another storyteller. The observant, curious and sympathetic eyes of Woon reveals a Balji beyond the byline. As a student, practitioner and teacher of journalism, I have always found Balji highly professional, thought provoking and often with an oblique angle that eluded others. He was both a speaker and a subject in my classes. Balji's own book was a critical contribution to a rather slim collection of journalism literature on Singapore media. Woon's book on Balji is a welcome addition to the even thinner layer of biographies of Singaporean journalists.

With the advent of personal mass media, better known as Social Media, traditional journalism has lost much of its appeal as the most important source of information on and analysis of public affairs. However, there is an aspect of traditional journalism that is critically needed today – journalism values. They go beyond timeliness and factual accuracy. Integrity and independence are most needed today in the face of an onslaught of misinformation and disinformation.

Singapore traditional media, like Singapore itself, is a mixed blessing. While adequate in craft and adept at technology, journalism values of integrity and independence have not been its badge of honour. This is where this book on Balji, along with those written by himself, Cheong Yip Seng and Cherian George – all previous stalwarts of traditional media – are invaluable in understanding the struggles of honest-to-good journalists to earn their reputation as well as their keep. Balji's life beyond the keyboard tells of a life lived with values. If such values do not drive traditional journalism, we would have neither good traditions nor good journalism in our country.

Arun Mahizhnan

Special Research Adviser, Institute of Policy Studies;
Former Adjunct Professor, Wee Kim Wee School of
Communication & Information, NTU

TRANSITION
The Story of PN Balji

A celebration of multi-generational Singapore.

Preface

It was a spur-of-the-moment hug, uninhibited, visceral and joyful. Arrian, then eight years old, held on to his grandpa in a mirthful embrace that would have made any Hollywood or Bollywood director very happy – a perfect shot. Thankfully, someone with a mobile phone handy had snapped at the right moment. It was Balji's birthday, his face was hidden by the boy's, leaving his expression to the imagination but the grandson's face said it all. Showing perfect white teeth, his handsome young face was both protective and celebratory, one could almost feel his youthful pull, with both his arms fully wrapped around the upper girth of his grandfather.

It was one of those moments we witness way too often in the movies, but not near enough in real life. Spontaneous, happy hugs are rare, especially in Asia. It attests to an intimate familiarity, one where the boy knows instinctively that the embrace will be appreciated and returned.

This photograph, taken in Kerala in India, captures the spirit of this book, a celebration of multi-generational Singapore. From young journalist to husband, then father and now grandfather, Balji's perspective as a Singapore native is considered, bold and always original. The narrative is charmed by a self-taught entrepreneur wife with a family of print, online and broadcast journalists. Made abundantly clear by this photo, there is plenty of love around this family, unravelling beautifully from a home Balji bought nearly 50 years ago, on Clover Way.

The book begins with an introductory dialogue with Balji, setting out conversationally the scope of the book. The answers to the questions also capture the man, who is first and foremost a family man. The public knows PN Balji as a political commentator and a media veteran with a gift for simple and effective prose. Behind the deceptively simple English is also a man steeped in the Malayalam and Tamil languages and cultures, a traditional husband with a liberal touch, a night editor who rushed home in time to see his daughter off to school, and a friend some trust their lives with.

I started writing this book unsure of where it would take me. I just knew instinctively that in Balji and his family, there was a Singapore story to tell. I meet Balji on Monday mornings, as one would with friends. And through the weeks and months, I tried hard to keep these meetings to Mondays, for no other reason than to create a routine. I believe regularity and familiarity have a way of engendering original thoughts and ideas, and also triggering memories, especially during the fresh early hours over steaming cups of *kopi*.

From these cool Monday mornings fuelled with aromatic coffee, I have been able to draw out personal accounts of "Identity", how an Indian man in love with his home state of Kerala develops an intense love-hate relationship with Singapore. The difficult concept of "Roots", how practical and easy Singapore has allowed his children and grandchildren to set up home so deep that poor but culturally rich India struggles to keep up. And then the elephant in the room – Singapore. Compared to India, the very concept of Singapore as a country and nation is still up for grabs. With social media, everyone has an opinion and with the pandemic, the opinions and views get increasingly fractious and even xenophobic. It

Mondays with Balji.

is here that Balji is in his element, his perspective buttressed by a lifetime of talking to laymen and women, harvested as much from the ground as it is gleaned from the top.

The future of media and the future of Singapore are never far from Balji's mind and they come through strongly here, chapter after chapter. Whether it is the reorganisation of the money-losing Singapore Press Holdings or the botched leadership transition in Singapore, his steely analyses and forecasts in *The New Singapore*, his weekly online column, are closely followed by netizens. Some of his thoughts there are reproduced in the Annex of this book.

The central narrative of this book captures what Balji is obsessed with today, the concept of family and home in contemporary Singapore. As he adjusts into his role as granddad, he is instructed by the demands of the modern family and what the younger generation is occupied with. And now, retired from a full-time job, he has time to look at his home with a more critical eye. Does Singapore really care for the needs of its citizens, especially the older generation? As a people, have we lost sight of our grace and civility? Through the prism of modern Singapore, a confusing sense of alienation has seeped in. Balji asks, if home is where one receives sustenance, is invited and welcomed into, is Singapore still home?

Introduction

A conversation with PN Balji

You have been a journalist in Singapore for more than 40 years. Have you been hauled up by the authorities for doing things they didn't like? The proverbial midnight knock on the door, perhaps?

There were two occasions when that feared knock happened. The first involved *The New Paper*'s crime reporter, Suresh Nair, who had received some inside information about the crash of the Super Puma helicopter at Sembawang Air Base in 1991. Four people died. The statement from the Ministry of Defence (Mindef) was, as always, very brief. Suresh, excellent at ferreting out details, dug up a lot more information from his sources, including the likely cause of the crash. It was one year into my editorship and Suresh was at the top of his game. In our eagerness to get the story out, we did not pay enough attention to the fact that we were contravening Mindef regulations. The ministry ordered an investigation to find out who had leaked the story to the media. Suresh and I were asked to meet then Permanent Secretary of Defence, Lim Siong Guan, who demanded that we name our sources. We declined and told Lim that if we named the sources, then we might as well stop being journalists as nobody would talk to us again.

A week later, we were called in again. Again, Lim asked us to identify Suresh's sources, and again we declined. Later, we were told we would be charged in court for contravening Mindef regulations. For some strange reason, that didn't happen, but the sources who gave Suresh the details were found out and they paid a heavy price. Some were sacked, others demoted. It was an incident that haunts us even today. Nothing happened to the journalists, but the sources were punished. When similar stories came to my attention, I was particularly careful in fudging the details which we hoped would protect our sources.

Fourteen years later, a similar case cropped up. I had moved to *TODAY* and another newshound, Jose Raymond, had a tip off that the RSS Courageous had met with an accident and four Republic of Singapore Navy officers were dead. He had all the details, like what time the accident happened, how many died, where it happened. My Super Puma experience kicked in and I told Jose to blur some of the details such that the Navy could not pin us down with its rules. We were proven right. The authorities did not come down hard on us.

Suresh was the star of another controversy. This time it was the literal dreaded midnight knock on the door. Late one night, a number of Corrupt Practices Investigation Bureau (CPIB) officers went to his home and took him away. He and his wife were terrified. Suresh was interrogated for many hours: the officers wanted to know if he had bribed Central Narcotics Bureau officers to get his stories. He denied the allegations. Suresh was shaken and asked to be moved out of crime reporting altogether. We heard nothing about it after that and no charges were brought against him. It dawned on me that CPIB took Suresh in to frighten him. He was so worked up that he asked for a transfer to the sub-editor's desk. The tactic worked – CPIB won.

Getting into trouble with the authorities – was that something that was always on your mind?

Scoops are what journalists live for. This was especially so for most of the publications I was involved in; they were underdogs, struggling to climb up the banyan tree for some sunlight. Getting exclusives in a country like Singapore, where information is so hard to get, a reporter worth his salt will push the boundaries. But he then runs the risk of stepping on the toes of the men in power and angering the authorities. My job as editor of underdog newspapers was to encourage my reporters to go for the scoop, but to make sure they didn't fall foul of the law. It was a tough balancing act. Yes, it was always at the back of my mind.

Did you discuss what might have happened to you with your wife and family?

Not all the time; no point alarming them unnecessarily. My yardstick was this: if I felt an issue would break out into the public domain, I would tell them. It would have been bad for them to learn of my misfortune from reports in the media.

You were the editor of publications in both SPH and MediaCorp, and helmed them over the period when three Prime Ministers were in charge of Singapore. Who impressed you most?

There is a chapter in my book titled, "*TODAY* Bets on Goh Chok Tong". Goh described himself as "An improbable Prime Minister for an unlikely country" in his book, *Tall Order*,[1] and was once famously described as "wooden" by his boss, Lee Kuan Yew, in his communication skills. Except for his imposing height, he was an ordinary man. Yet, he succeeded in being a well-liked PM. He found in himself strengths and political skills he did not know he had. To step out of Lee Kuan Yew's shadow was no mean feat, but he did it. When we started *TODAY* in 2000, we wanted to fill an editorial gap in the market – the intention was to be bold and to inject analysis into our news reports, the "why" of the news, not just the "who", "what", "where" and "how". Would the Singapore government be amenable to this type of journalism? Lee Kuan Yew and his key ministers had spoken out publicly on many occasions against mixing news with analyses and comments. I was confident Goh, who was into his tenth year as PM, wanted to move away from Lee Kuan Yew's shadow and would not interfere with our editorial thrust. Not once in my three-year editorship of *TODAY* was there a call from the PM's office to complain about our style of reporting.

Have you given in to any government demands?
Many times, too often to count. Most of the government demands and requests came via the editor-in-chief. It was very difficult for us to not follow the orders/requests once he had agreed to them.

In all the stories you have done, as journalist or editor, which is the one which brought the greatest hurt to those affected?
When I was the editor of *The New Paper* from 1990 to 2000, sports was our main focus. And soccer was the national pasttime then. It happened that my brother, Sivaji, was the coach of the national team. I saw this as a conflict of interest. I went to the editor-in-chief, telling him that I would recuse myself from having any say in reports of the matches he was involved in. Cheong Yip Seng said he trusted my judgement

and he was sure that I would be impartial. To appear to be whiter than white, I went the other way and told the reporters to criticise him every step of the way. It was an error of judgement on my part and much later, I realised how unfair I had been to my brother. After he quit as coach, I wrote him an apology letter which I wanted to include in my book, *Reluctant Editor*.[2] But for a variety of reasons, it wasn't in the book. This is something I would have to take to my grave. It pains me each time I think of it.

Who was or is one person who most impressed you in your journalistic career?

Peter Lim. He tried to hold the ground when he felt government demands were unreasonable. But he was not fundamental. When the editor-in-chief felt the government was reasonable, he played ball. One of his actions, in 1981, continues to make many of us who worked with him proud to be journalists. *The Straits Times* had responded publicly to then Communications and Labour Minister, Ong Teng Cheong, who criticised it and *New Nation* for publishing what he called "irresponsible, misleading and rumour-mongering" reports on an impending bus fare hike. The reporters attributed the information to unnamed sources. As group editor, Peter Lim went public with a spirited defence of the newspapers and their reporters. It was a public defence I have not witnessed since. I was then the acting editor of *New Nation* and was present at the press conference that Ong had called to deny the reports. Key ministry officials and Singapore Bus Service bosses were also there. The minister demanded that we name our sources and one of them was there sitting right in front of us. Peter declined, saying that professional ethics prevented him from naming names, and he also conceded that the sources, though authoritative, had now proven unreliable.

As I said, that incident was a rare moment in Singapore's press history and that day I was proud to be a Singapore journalist. We learned from Peter Lim how the media could respond when it felt it had been unjustly reprimanded by the government. He responded unemotionally and fairly.

There were many other occasions when he stood up for his staff or to protect the credibility of his papers. One more example was in the 1984 election, when PAP candidate Mah Bow Tan was introduced as a candidate, and his rival was Singapore Democratic Party's Chiam See Tong in Potong Pasir. Lee Kuan Yew revealed at an election rally the top-line exam results of both candidates to show that the Opposition man was not so smart. Later in the day, Lee wanted *The Straits Times* to publish the detailed results of the two men. Peter's position was that, if the PM had disclosed the full exam results during the rally, he would use them. Otherwise, using the new information would not be good for the government and *The Straits Times*. Lee's press secretary called Peter several times to persuade Peter to change his mind. But Peter stood firm.

The cumulative effect of Peter's belief that the media in Singapore should be given room to disagree occasionally ultimately cost him his job as editor-in-chief in December 1986. He had been in the job for only eight years. Today, I remember him for his acts of independence and selfless leadership. He was one of a kind.

What is the hardest part of being married?
Probably the hardest part was coming to terms with the partnership and the realisation of how the person I had married has changed over time. When I met my wife, she was young and innocent. Over the years, the person changes. Today, Uma is an independent woman, capable and speaks her mind. It hasn't been easy to adjust to the changes. But that is also the most satisfying part. I am happy for my wife, and how marriage has given her a new lease on life, how she has seized it and made the most of it. If something happens to me, she'd be okay. I know someone who, when she lost her husband, was completely lost. I wouldn't want that to happen to my wife. I made sure that she would become independent and not need me as a crutch.

Cite an incident or event you most treasure about a friend.
His name is Pasupathy and he was working for SPH in the production department. Curiously, he was also a moneylender and charged interest for the amounts he loaned. When I bought my home in Clover Way more than 40 years ago, I was short of money to pay for the deposit. I went to him and told him I needed $10,000. I had just started out and was a young journalist. Money was in short supply. He not only gave me the money but said I didn't have to pay him any interest. It was a kind act I will not forget. An angel dressed in moneylender's clothes.

What makes you feel most alive?
When I write or read a good story. Watching my grandsons grow. There was a card game we played, where everyone had to name his or her favourite book. Mine was *Jonathan Livingston*

Seagull.[3] Both my grandsons said *Reluctant Editor* by their granddad. Moments like these make me feel most alive.

What makes you feel most vulnerable?
The thought that something could happen to those close to me, if something happens to my wife, children or grandchildren. If any one of them gets into an accident, suffers an illness or emotional distress, I would feel vulnerable.

What is the best advice you've ever given?
My youngest daughter met a man, and after a while he asked her hand in marriage. She was not sure and asked for my advice. I told her to be calm and list down all his good and bad points. Then look at the list and ask herself if she could live with them. She had a problem with his smoking habit. I remember telling her smoking wasn't a character trait and she could influence him to quit. He is now her husband. And he continues to smoke.

NOTES

1   Peh Shing Huei, *Tall Order: The Goh Chok Tong Story* (World Scientific, 2018).

2   PN Balji, *Reluctant Editor – The Singapore Media as Seen Through the Eyes of a Veteran Newspaper Journalist* (Marshall Cavendish Editions, 2019).

3   Richard Bach, *Jonathan Livingston Seagull* (Macmillan, 1970); reissued as *Jonathan Livingston Seagull: The Complete Edition* in 2014.

Balji in his Naval Base
Primary School uniform,
1957.

Family portrait,
Balji (left) with
parents, sister and
brother, 1957.

Chapter 1

On Clover Way

Building the foundation: marriage and family

The gentleman caller

The commute from Novena to Bishan is just three stops, it takes a mere 15 minutes on the train. But the walk from the station to 27 Clover Way is another 15. And that's the best part of the journey, walking through the private estate of landed homes in Singapore. Bungalows, semi-detached or terraced houses, Singapore's landed property has the rare distinction of being completely eclectic.

In a row of 25 terraced houses, one is likely to see 25 different architectural approaches to tropical living. Almost every landed home would have been renovated at one time or another, and each tries to maximise the living space sidewards and also upwards. There is little or no regard for the architectural traditions of the neighbourhood nor is there a need to fit in with what the immediate neighbours have done. Each household stretches its interior and exterior architectural potential to the limit, a creative exercise of trying to make the most out of a small piece of land. Foreigners are generally not allowed to buy landed property, and given how scarce and expensive land is, landed homes are priced at a premium, a unique Singapore phenomenon, occupying a slice of the middle and upper-middle enclaves of Singapore.

I had texted Uma, Balji's wife, earlier in the week for an appointment, asking if she knew of a relaxing cafe in the neighbourhood where we could meet.

"Why not 27 Clover Way?" she replied simply.

"Can. Not a problem." I wanted privacy from her husband, since we would, invariably, be talking about him. But she would know better, and the house is probably big enough for a private chat. Or he could have a cup of coffee at the corner coffee shop on Clover Way.

En route to 27 Clover Way, I pause at 91, a corner terrace house my brother had bought almost 30 years ago. We stayed there for only a couple of years. The place seems small and sad now, the current owner hasn't done much to cheer it up. My mother was still relatively young and active when we had all stayed there, our first years without our father, who had passed just before we moved. My memories of 91 Clover Way are anxiety-filled and sad like the place. The bedroom I slept in faces the park and has a balcony. It's peculiar, but I have no memory of ever looking out to enjoy the view.

In sharp contrast to 91, 27 Clover Way emanates positive energy almost from the moment I enter the gate. Two ivory white elephants stand guard on top of the pillars on each side of the entrance. Quietly regal, they welcome guests with an attentive knowing. Elephants are of course highly revered in Indian culture, and especially in the Hindu religion. Lord Ganesha is said to be a remover of obstacles and a provider of fortune and good luck. The mythological Hindu beliefs have established elephants as sacred symbols of peace, mental strength and power.

And these energies are in abundance as I walk in. The house has been recently renovated but it does not seem unfamiliar or awkward. Even though the alterations are relatively major, there is a sense somehow that the new has the permission of the old to be here, and have taken over with ease and confidence. Unlike some other landed homes, this house has kept the integrity of its original design, the changes are strategic and not showy, and it is practical, modern and clean.

"It took several months, the renovation, but it was worth it," says Uma. Hers is a low timbered voice, not unlike that of a commentator in broadcast. Every word is enunciated, but the emphasis is subtle and unforced. "My daughter suggested hiring an interior decorator. But I knew what I wanted and I knew my contractors well. Together I was sure we could come up with something satisfactory."

Satisfactory. The self-taught designer has a knack of playing down what she has single-handedly achieved. Without formal training, just a keen eye for design, she has quietly pulled off an architectural coup. The main door is generous, wider than before. It has two vertical strips of glass on both sides to let the light in and, more importantly, allow those inside to see who the visitors are without opening the door. The windows are broader and shorter versions of the strip look, giving the entire living room a clean, modern feel. The biggest change to the place is a large "cut-out opening" of the main wall of the stairs. Encased in a simple gold border, it functions as the decorative centerpiece of the house. Not only does it allow a peek into the stairs going up, it psychologically broadens the living space, giving it the required expansive, "wall-less" feel. The dining room has a washing area that is semi-hidden. At the back of the house where the kitchen is located, the wall-less motif continues; it accommodates another sitting area and a makeshift "bedroom", in case both husband and wife can't climb the stairs to sleep in the bedroom on the second level.

At five foot two, or perhaps three, her face is always on the brink of a smile, and there is a fillip to her gait, signs of a contented person. She makes tea with milk and heats up a slice of pie from the fridge. Although I have many questions in mind, I know my focus this Wednesday morning is on her arranged marriage that happened more than 40 years ago. Uma is 63 years old, born in Taiping, Malaysia. After the race riots in 1969, her father had sent the entire family to Kerala, India. The year was 1973, she was 18 and looking forward to college. In her own words, she was "too young" to take anything seriously. Then, like most girls her age in India, the ideal man was one of those she had seen in the movies, or better yet, Tarzan from Hollywood films. When a gentleman caller came visiting with his mother for tea one afternoon, she didn't think much of it. That he would be her future husband was the furthest thing on her mind. No one told her that her world, as she knew it, was about to change.

"He was big ... fat, actually, and looked stern with curly hair," she remembers with a straight face. Even though she did not "meet" him, she caught glimpses of him from the safety of her bedroom upstairs. And the big man didn't say a word. Later, she found out that the man and his mother had come for the hand of her second sister, only to discover that she was already engaged. They were told that the third daughter, Uma, was available. It all seemed destined today, but nothing was real to her then, even when that "meeting" lasted almost two hours.

"He did not look anything like a movie star, and Tarzan he was not. He was more like a hippie," says Uma, with mirth in her big dark eyes. "I was young and was, of course, disappointed that he wanted to marry me. In fact, quite a few people around me were surprised that I was to be married to him."

The big man and his mother went away, saying they would come back with an answer. But no word came. Young Uma was secretly relieved. Weeks turned into months and everyone thought the proposed marriage was off. But after almost half a year later, word finally came. The big man wanted to go ahead with the marriage after all.

As marriage plans started to roll out, Uma finally had an inkling that her life would change soon. The first casualty was college, she had to put her college plans on hold. "I was young, I went along with what was planned, I tried not to focus on my future husband, I didn't know what marriage would entail. I only focused on one person, and that was his mother. When he came with his mother, I liked her instantly, even from afar. I could tell that she was kind and, somehow, I knew things wouldn't be so bad with her around."

As the days passed, marriage loomed as an impending reality. Her future husband tried to bring her out on a date once, but her father said no. Her family was traditional and strict; like her first and second sisters before her, there would be no dating. They did speak a few times on the phone, very short conversations, perhaps for five minutes each time at the most.

Being close to her first sister, she exchanged notes with her on what to expect from the man she would call husband. Some details, like what she needed to do on her wedding night, shocked her. It was a glimpse into the future as a wife, but it also consoled her to know that she would be a woman and mother as a result. As the big day drew closer, she prepared herself mentally. He was a big man, so much bigger than her, and she needed to think of him differently. A few things became clear to her by now: even though her father lived in Malaysia and the marriage would take place there, she would be joining her future husband in the southern city of Singapore. There, she would be staying with his brother, nieces and parents. They would be one big family. She was secretly relieved that she would not be left alone with her future husband.

Confirmation, preparation and invitations for the big day took all of one month. The wedding was in Taiping, a historical and cultural town in northwest Malaysia. Because everything happened so fast, the wedding wasn't as elaborate as most Indian weddings, but an Indian wedding was still an Indian wedding. The focus was on the ceremonial event at the temple. There, the highlight of the ceremony was when sliced banana dipped in milk was fed to the bridegroom and the bride with the same spoon. It was a ceremonial "permission" to have sex.

"There were so many people, strangers to me, people I didn't know," she says, sounding a little surprised that she remembers such details after more than 40 years. "Slowly, everything became more real, in front of all those strangers, it was becoming clearer to me that the man sitting next to me was going to be the most important man in my life." She remembers whispers in her ear that he seemed and looked fierce, that he was large and unfriendly, but at the ceremony, she experienced a new calm and she remembers thinking to herself that she was not afraid. She blocked out the crowds, the noise and focused on just her new path forward, as a wife. The ceremonial wedding was over within the hour, and she emerged from it clear-eyed and ready. Her gut feeling told her she would be fine.

The first night proved to be uneventful at Balji's sister's place. There were two single beds, separated. They barely talked. The real "conversations" happened on their honeymoon, away from everyone at Cameron Highlands. With the hullabaloo and stress of the wedding behind them, there was something crisp and new in the air between them. No shouts or whispers, no fussing, no instructions, just the two of them. Bit by youthful bit, she allowed the tension of the wedding to slowly slip away. And she realised, as the days passed blissfully by, that the big man was actually a gentle man and, more importantly, a kind man. Mr Hippie was serious, attentive and respectful. So, her gut feel was right after all. The first lesson she learned on her honeymoon was that while people could tell her things, she would have to verify them herself, especially when they concerned this man, Balji, whom she now called her husband. Quite suddenly, she was getting used to being Mrs Balji. Their union had been conceived in the womb of trust and hope. Now, this nourishing environment gave them both a new life.

And, unknown to her, marriage would be her "college", her greatest education. It would be a journey to becoming a good wife and a good mother, and later a good grandmother. And unknown to her, too, marriage would also unleash the businesswoman in her, and she would be the unofficial CFO of her household. And to top all, the big man whose features were round and obtuse would become slimmer and sharper with age. She also did not know it then, that a humble terrace house along Clover Way would become her most important base.

The couple's traditional wedding ceremony, 1973.

Getting to know each other.

Private and public lives

As usual, I am early. The January morning air is moist from a full day and night of rain. The coffee shop at the corner of Clover Way looks warm, inviting and very full. Even at this early hour, every table is taken. A waitress looks from the corner of her eye, then resumes making coffee. Another catches my attention with a point of her index finger – ah, over there, an empty table at the back. Her eyes smile, or they appear to. These days, I try to read eye expressions as half of everyone's face is masked.

"*Kopi c kosong.*" I have switched to black coffee with evaporated milk, no sugar. A first step in my journey to cut out sugar in my diet, a tip from Balji.

The unsmiling eyes of the waitress look straight into mine as she says, "$1.20." Her body language is negative, her tone unattractive; something tells me it comes from an equally unattractive face. I try hard not to take a dislike to someone on my first encounter.

The coffee is bitterly wonderful, just what I need at this early hour. From the drone of the radio, the Chinese news repeats what has been reported the night before: Nancy Pelosi says the Democrats will proceed with impeachment proceedings against President Donald Trump. The clouds lay low, threatening to rain. I notice Balji walking towards the coffee shop. With a full head of wavy grey hair, Balji carries his lithe physique with casual ease. Although he has had his fair share of health scares, he looks a decade younger than 72, every step has the bounce of a carefree man, his eyes wearing an ever-ready smile.

A table is now empty at the balcony. "Let's sit there," I say as I walk towards the front. "Better here, the radio is way too loud at the back."

"So, you finished your book." Balji pulls off his mask and his face breaks into a smile. He is one of those lucky people blessed with facial features that is enhanced with age. I had asked him to write a blurb for my recently completed book on artist Lim Tze Peng. "It's a good book, I remember writing a blurb for your book on Tan Swie Hian. This is better." Coming from a bestselling author, I am grateful.

Then, without warning, I feel a physical presence next to me. The mouth of a waitress is inches away from my face. "The doctor says my arteries are blocked," she whispers in Mandarin, her eyes fixed on Balji's face.

"Gangsta Sista! Meet my friend, Tai Ho." Balji is a regular at the coffee shop and knows practically everyone here, and he has a colourful nickname for every waitress. He seems especially close to the two waitresses who are now jostling for his attention.

"She has seen the doctor and it's not good news, her arteries are blocked." I repeat in English what she has just said. Gangsta Sista postures, her big body reacts awkwardly, the bashfulness of a young girl.

Balji seems concerned but distracted, he waves at the other waitress at the back. "Mama-san!" he calls out playfully. Gangsta Sista looks around and walks back to the counter, ignoring the other waitress, or Mama-san as Balji has just called her. Tense. One can cut the air of rivalry between the two waitresses with a knife.

"They don't get along," says Balji, looking away from the waitresses. "It's sad, they work in the same place but refuse to talk to each other. Each will come to me and complain about the other."

It doesn't surprise me that he is friendly to the employees in a coffee shop. In all the years that I have known him – coming up to 20 – Balji has always gravitated towards the support staff or those who form the lower strata of the workforce: interns, tea ladies, secretaries, drivers and foreign workers. These workers do not enjoy the company of the powerful, but they know sentiments from the ground, unfiltered and organic feelings, and gossip very often absent at the middle or the top. It shows the journalist in him, a mind that says the best sources are the hands and legs of a place, not necessarily the head. I recall once looking at Balji talking to a foreign worker, and it reminded me of Finley Peter Dunn's declaration that the duty of a newspaper is to comfort the afflicted, and afflict the comfortable.

"So, will Trump be impeached?" On Wednesday, 6 January, supporters of President Donald Trump stormed the US Capitol building in Washington DC while Congress voted to certify President-elect Joe Biden's victory. The unprecedented event echoed across the world, prompting calls for the resignation and impeachment of the president. As always, I know Balji has a view, a considered view.

"It probably won't happen; it would cause unrest, which is what Trump wants." Balji seems tired of a topic that has gripped the world media in the last few days. Instead, his focus is on the hot local topic, the TraceTogether crisis. "I've just completed a piece for *Yahoo News* on why no one in government spotted the flaw in Vivian Balakrishnan's promise that TraceTogether data would only be used for contact tracing."

And so our first Monday meeting takes off, like most meetings, with world and local news taking center stage. I remind myself that this Monday meeting is the first of many other Monday meetings. "Mondays with Balji" will now be a weekly routine for us – yes, we can talk about anything under the tropical sun, but as the author, I need to subtly direct the conversation.

During a lunch to celebrate his birthday in December, I had broached the topic about a book. Balji's first book, *Reluctant Editor*, published in 2019, was a non-fiction bestseller. It took the reader through the five newspapers he had worked in and highlighted the challenges and successes he experienced. It showcased a large part of his professional life but in my mind, however, that was just one part of his story. There is so much more yet to be covered.

It occurred to me that a writer may find it odd to write about himself in a book. When does a writer stop before his narrative becomes boastful? Who tells the writer when he is being too modest? And when does a piece of writing become too subjective, involved or personal? But if the narrative is written by an observer, the situation shifts subtly. And as a friend and observer of Balji for so long, I think there is a lot to be said about Balji the husband, the father and now the grandfather. And more importantly, what are his innermost feelings about the country he grew up in?

When we submit an application for a job, we make sure our qualifications and relevant experiences are in order. Which school we attended, the grades obtained and the years invested in relevant organisations play a big role in the chances of getting the job. But we have no say in who our parents are; and in Balji's case, who his wife would be in an arranged marriage. We view this part of our lives as being private, even if a lot of it is public knowledge. One could be a brilliant CEO, making a ton of money for the company, but the same CEO could also be an absent husband and father. Our spouses, children and grandchildren will grade us eventually. How happy or lonely we are in old age says something about how successful we have been in our private lives.

They call it the school of life, where there are no textbooks, no examinations. The consequences of each step are often not immediately apparent, the chickens coming home to roost only much later, and very often played out in ways that cannot be reversed. When nothing is scripted, most of us borrow the compass of our elders, following the successful paths of those before us, sometimes even when they are no longer relevant or useful. Then there are those, like Balji, who have managed to write their own scripts, and with remarkable outcomes.

I write this book to distil what I think is precious to know and understand. In observing and occasionally participating in the "private" life of Balji, I have come to understand and respect the institutions of marriage and family, two areas that have gone through the most dramatic changes in the contemporary world. In the fast passage of time, too many things change, and with a rapidity that is muddling and confusing. It is calming and reassuring to see how some individuals have not only preserved but also innovated these institutions to stay relevant, meaningful and, yes, even happy.

All this in a country that is younger than Balji. Independent Singapore is all of 57 years old, and over these past five decades, from separation to independence, breaking away from the colonial yoke, attracting foreign investment, becoming a First World country, Singapore has punched above its size and done well. And Balji has rolled with the punches.

Today, many of the early assumptions of Singapore are being questioned by an increasingly international and critical citizenry. This young country has looked within and asks, are we on the correct path? Are there too many foreigners? Are we divided along racial lines? Is a one-party governed country what we want? Is the Opposition strong enough to keep the ruling party in check? Balji has been at the forefront of these questions, and here in this book, his answers are heartfelt and personal. He emphasises, often, that he is pro-Singapore, not necessarily pro-PAP nor pro-Opposition.

Again, I feel someone just inches away from me.

"You want to order something to eat?" Gangsta Sista pushes a not-so-clean menu onto the table, next to my empty coffee cup. There is a wink in her voice.

Balji smiles, "The *nasi lemak* is good here."

The sky has cleared up. A cyan-blue sky breaks through the clouds and Gangsta Sista's eyes beam.

"I'll have the *nasi lemak*." I am ready to eat.

First memories

I was introduced to Balji when he was the editor of *TODAY* at MediaCorp Press in 2000, the year I launched Channel NewsAsia. Then, like now, Balji spoke in a confident, unforced manner that was disarming. But if you don't know him, he can be intimidating. Until he smiles or shows an interest in a conversation, Balji comes across at times as unfriendly, even cold and aloof. In a work environment, he does not talk much, and prefers to scan from a discreet corner. And when he chooses to speak, what comes out is usually thought through, spoken slowly and deliberately. His whole professional persona is work-focused, or as someone says, "All quiet intellectuals are scary." And with Balji, there is the added current affairs knowledge. A journalist his entire life, his gaze is news empowered, his conversations are laced with the latest facts. It is difficult to have a "casual" chat with him, until he chooses to be casual himself.

This week, I meet him in the afternoon at 4pm, same place, the corner coffee shop. The place is relatively empty in the afternoon and as we settle down in the balcony taking the same seats as we did the week before, Mama-san is getting ready to leave. Another waitress attends to us.

"Gigi, my friend wants this too," Balji points to his *chee cheong fun*, a Cantonese rice noodle roll served with seasoned soy sauce.

"And a *teh c kosong*." I decide to have tea with evaporated milk, no sugar. Gigi, a smaller and younger waitress, nods.

Today, we decide to begin at the beginning, and the beginning for Balji is his marriage; this time, I get to hear his version of it. He begins by lamenting about the state of marriage in contemporary Singapore. "We have heard this before – let me get my life in order first, get a good job and I'll think about marriage," he says, imitating a young woman we both know. "And the potential husband? Oh, I need to know everything about him before we take the plunge. Why? Because it is the most important decision in our lives! So, most marriages happen in their 30s, even 40s. Not good, especially for the women. What to do? This is the reality today."

How different it was 40 years ago! Then, everyone entered the institution of marriage without a map. It was a generation that didn't expect so much of each other and probably ended up getting more. Yes, we are talking about arranged marriages. When he was introduced to his wife-to-be in 1973, he tried to ask if he could take her out on a date. His request was denied outright. And in less than six months, they were married: engaged in September and married in October that year. The bride and groom walked into the marital bedroom scented with faith and hope – theirs was a commitment to explore and get to know each other in their lifetime. Breakups and divorces were not common, the approach was to enter the union and make it work. Today, it is difficult for Balji to think of a time when he wasn't married to Uma, and every major decision in their lives is made together.

As the afternoon cools off, Balji remembers a detail of their engagement. "It took place at a friend's house in Novena," Balji starts. "The conversation was about dowry, and in the case of our culture, it is an amount of property or money brought by a bride to her husband on their marriage. Uma came from a rich family; her father gave handsome dowries for his first two daughters." Balji stops, his brows lifting high dramatically. "My father, being the socialist that he was, asks, 'Is this a fish market?' That put a stop to all the dowry talk." There is pride seething through him as he leans back. "In the early years when the going got tough, I wished I had the dowry, but looking back, I am proud of my father. He forced me to be the self-made man that I am."

Then, another detail. Uma could not see it herself, but Balji noticed a birthmark just below the back of her neck soon after their marriage. The Indians believe that when a birthmark cannot be seen by the individual, it is a good sign. Balji, although not a superstitious man, allowed himself the luxury to believe that it was a good sign for him and their marriage. Like the mark that could not be seen, an arranged marriage was one that relied almost entirely on faith at the start, faith that the journey ahead would be filled with good discoveries of each other, and if there were to be surprises, they would be good ones, too.

They started out on their lives together living in Sembawang Hills estate with his parents, brother and nieces. The house at 114 Nemesu Avenue, in the Ang Mo Kio vicinity, was comfortable but not his own home. After their first daughter Deepa was born, it was clear to him that they needed their own space, a house of their own, one they could call home.

"I looked in the newspapers and saw a house along Clover Way for sale," Balji says, looking at the neighbourhood, remembering. "The original house I wanted was $4,000 more, so I bought number 27 because it was available. There was no science or logic to buying a place, it just happened. Clover Way was the only place I looked. I paid a $50 deposit." It was a $97,000 decision; in the present day, one would not be able to buy a decent car with that amount, but it was quite a lot of money in the 1970s. He asked his boss, Peter Lim, for a housing loan, even though he knew *The Straits Times* did not give housing loans to its staff. So when the loan came through, he knew his boss had made a special case for him. He did not know it then, but Peter Lim would become a lifelong friend, one who was instrumental in some key decisions he would make in his career.

When we are done with our coffee, Balji invites me back to his house. The two ivory elephants guarding the gate seem to recognise me, I imagine them moving their long trunks agreeably towards me. I like entering 27 Clover Way, it has a way of humouring my whims without making a show of it.

"Almost everything you see here is designed by Uma and made in Kerala," Balji says with understated pride from the main sitting area in the living room. Being house proud takes on a different meaning when every corner has been filled with home comforts personally designed by the owner and put together by craftsmen in Kerala, their other home in India.

Of course, it wasn't like this when they first moved in. In fact, when the couple and their daughter first moved in, they slept on the floor without mattresses, that was how much Balji wanted to have a place of his own, even though his job didn't pay well and the future was anything but certain. The home was built, quite literally, piece by painstaking piece.

"When we left Nemesu Avenue, my mother cried. It was tough but I was determined to be on my own, be with my own family," says Balji. It is difficult to tell if he is emotionless or emotional, as his face betrays nothing. "I arrived in Clover Way with just one suitcase."

Balji is more expressive when it comes to a painful episode on Clover Way. In those early days working for *The Straits Times*, when he was the night editor, work was not just hard and frustrating, but his shifts also ended late. Most nights, he and his colleagues would adjourn to Newton Hawker Centre, these sessions being the highlight of the workday, after putting the newspaper to bed. On one of those nights, supper included drinking and it lasted until early morning at 5.30am. By the time he drove back home it was dawn, late (or early enough) for him to catch a glimpse of his daughter, Deepa, waiting for the school bus. It was a heartbreaking moment. He was angry that he was late, guilty that he went out drinking, sorry that he couldn't see her off ... And that was the last time he was late. Henceforth, he would be home latest by two in the morning, sleep, then get up to see her off before he went back to sleep.

Today, 27 Clover Way has a huge open kitchen where Uma cooks. It is also here on the ground floor where a "bedroom" is located, "In case we find it hard to climb the stairs in old age," says Balji, realistically. His two grandchildren love the place because they have almost absolute freedom here – grandparents' rules are different from parents' rules. One of them, all of 13, even asked if he could buy the place.

"How much do I have to pay you?" he asks, like he is buying the latest computer game.

"Three million," says Balji. "But we have willed it to your mother and your aunt, you have to negotiate with them."

CFO

Her highest level of education was secondary or high school. And she didn't finish it because marriage was considered a priority, followed by husband, children, and then grandchildren.

"In my mind, I am always a wife," Uma says quietly, her low voice adding emphasis to the word *wife*. "And it's full time, it means knowing my husband's routine, his likes and dislikes, and the food, that's important." What happens when the children come? "Of course, you become a mother, but you don't stop being a wife. And when the grandchildren come, you become a grandmother, while you continue to be wife and mother."

So, when Uma takes on a new role, she does not discard the old ones. In her mind, the more she does, the better equipped she becomes. "When I learn a new skill like my ability to trade in the stock market, or understanding the property market, I don't see myself as a 'modern' woman who should discard household chores like cooking. I enjoy the kitchen too much."

I ask about the woman she has become today. She laughs and says: "We grow. I am no longer the innocent young girl from Kerala. I am lucky my husband allows me to be the woman I have become. Again, I hope I continue to be a good wife, a good mother and a good grandmother, in addition to whatever other labels people may want to tag on me, entrepreneur, property guru. They just describe what I also do, they do not cancel out all the roles that define me as a person."

When women become successful outside the kitchen, society has a tendency to write them off as liberators of traditions. But Uma does not see anything extraordinary about women achieving and doing well beyond traditional roles. "Again, I think I am lucky. There is no traditional roles and modern roles. I take care of my husband, I take care of my children, and now my grandchildren. And I do it my way. Outside of these, when I have time, I study the stock market, and watch out for opportunities in the property market."

Like her eye for design, she plays down what she achieves exceedingly well in investments. In the August 2005 issue of *Pulses*, a magazine which tracked the beat of Singapore's capital markets, Vasu Menon, who works for OCBC, called her "An Extraordinary Investor". The following is a short excerpt of the article. Uma provided the background to her investments in the Q & A feature.

I began to feel restless after my daughters grew up. I had a lot of spare time and so I decided to spend it reading about the local stock and property markets and investing in them.

Q: Are you a trader or an investor?

A: I am a bit of both. Among the stocks I have bought, I have held some for two years. As for the others, I sold them when they rose sharply and I was able to make fairly quick gains.

Q: How would you describe your track record? What were some of the best investment decisions you made?

A: I would say that my track record has been fairly good. While I have traded and invested in the local stock market, my best long-term investment decisions were made on properties and insurance endowment policies.

Q: Tell me more about your property investments?

A: My first foray into the property market took place sometime in the late 1980s. We bought an apartment in Upper Thomson for $370,000 and sold it less than six months later for $470,000. Soon after, I bought another apartment in Newton for $400,000 and sold it two years later for $600,000. Subsequently I purchased a property around Orchard Road area for $670,000 and sold it after ten years for $950,000. Almost immediately after I sold, I managed to purchase another unit in the same development for $850,000. I was able to spot investment opportunities in the property market because I watched it closely and did my homework before making my purchase.

That interview was done more than 15 years ago. Today, the property market is shrouded by restrictions. But Uma still keeps an eye on both stocks and property. "I like to do background research when I get interested in something,"

Uma begins. "And I was fascinated by the stock market. So I started reading up on some counters. Apart from reading the newspapers and relevant publications, I watch Bloomberg and CNBC. Over time, I knew enough about the market and important counters to start investing carefully. I told Balji and he was quite supportive."

What started off as just an interest became pretty "serious business": unlike the other things she was good at doing, this had a financial aspect to it. "Suddenly, she was making money," says Balji ironically. "I think she is good because she is cautious and bold at the same time. She is not reckless but when she needs to, she is remarkably tenacious and sees through what she started out with."

"Her temperament helps," says Deepa. "She is a steady and calm person, not easily rattled. Over time, she made money and had enough to hold during a difficult market. She does not need to 'cut her losses', so to speak. For the most part, she is a long-term player, although she also knows how to be opportunistic with good counters."

But the real money was in property. "When I make money in the stock market, the one place to put it in as real investment was and is property." Her first investment was an apartment in Faber Garden, an early condo development with complete facilities, pool, tennis and squash courts, ample car parks. It was a big development with sprawling land in Upper Thomson Road. The chances of anything going wrong were low. She could take a loan. So she committed. To her surprise, even before she contacted the bank for a loan, someone offered to buy it: she was offered a sum that would make her a profit of $300,000, net. After consulting with her husband, she sold. It was a fast paper transaction; she quickly learned that the person who had the guts to make the decision made the money. And so, over a span of 20 years, over a dozen transactions, she contributed to the financial stability of her household. Today, she still holds on to a couple of properties and they provide her and the family with good passive income.

Deepa, now in her 40s, thinks of her mother as a manager of funds. "My mother knows how busy Sri [her husband] and I are," she smiles. "She alerts me to good investment opportunities in the stock market and actually 'forces' us to buy properties as investment. Unlike my father who knew her first as a young woman, my image of her has always been someone capable, spiritually grounded and also the CFO of the house."

Coup

As we grow older, many memories come back to visit us, but flashes of images from our growing years tend to be the most recurring, affecting us, influencing us subliminally. Balji's most vivid image of his youth was that of his mother, her anxious face waiting by the balcony for him to get home from school. There are, of course, many other images of her in his mind, but somehow the one of her waiting, how she put everything aside to wait, has become indelible. Perhaps it was because of its repetition, it was recurring, same place, same time, every day. That image brings back everything else that comes with it: the feel of the hot afternoon sun, the musky humidity, him in his school uniform, and the quiet buzz of the flat in the Naval Base.

The date 1 February 2021 proves to be a surprise, a dramatic Monday morning. In Myanmar, a country I have spent two and a half years in, its people wake up to widespread Internet and communications blackouts, closed banks and soldiers in army fatigues patrolling the streets. In Yangon, Myanmar's biggest city, residents turning on their TV sets can only access the military-owned Myawaddy TV channel, with all other news channels seemingly blocked. As news filter through, the country's democratically-elected leaders, Aung San Suu Kyi and other senior government leaders, have been detained in the capital. A news anchor announces on the military-owned channel that power has been handed over to army chief Min Aung Hlaing.

Balji had visited me when I was in Myanmar in 2019, and we introduced his book, *Reluctant Editor*, to the Singaporeans living in Myanmar and a small group of media professionals in a small cafe in downtown Yangon. While he was there, I introduced him to a few of my close friends. But as expected, Balji became close to my driver, Saw, and my secretary, Koko. So, this Monday morning is a black Monday for the both of us. While we are curious about the political dynamics, we are more concerned about those we know in Yangon.

"So, why did it happen?" I ask, even though some reasons for the coup have been in the media. Perhaps Balji has a different take.

"The report from the BBC this morning was comprehensive." Balji is an admirer of the British Broadcasting Corporation's handling of the news, just as he is an avid admirer of the *Financial Times*. "The election results made the generals look bad. They are insecure, they won't let the government be formed based on those results."

I am glad I am out of Myanmar, but I keep thinking of Saw, Koko and my colleagues in Channel K, the entertainment channel I ran in Yangon. So far, no reports of civilian unrest, no arrest and no uprising. What would I be doing now if I were in Myanmar? Probably having breakfast across the road, and wondering if it is safe to go to the office; answering endless text messages from Singapore to tell everyone that I am safe and not to worry. There would also be the big question, should I get out of the country and return home to Singapore? "Do you think it will be back to the dark days of 1988?"

"Very possible. A perfect time for a coup when the entire world is caught up in a pandemic." Balji pauses, deep in thought.

"They don't care if foreign companies pull out," I think aloud.

"In the end, it's about power. They only care about power."

Enough distraction for one morning. Let me get back to Balji's story. This morning, I am focusing on his parents, beginning with his mother. "You are the first boy after five girls, it must have been a relief for your mother."

"For my mother, finally a boy after five girls. I was treated like a princeling." Balji says it matter-of-factly. No smile or a joke about how it felt then. I get the distinct feeling it was a time of his life he has mixed feelings about. Something seems to disturb him. "I was obese as a boy."

"You were obese?" I find that curious, knowing how careful Balji is with his diet today.

He shrugs. "My mother was loving," he says, then adds, "to a fault."

The early years for Balji were disturbing years, as it turned out. His mother wanted everyone in the family to stay together and would have done anything to keep it that way. Also, she was so loving that she hid the faults of her children.

His father was a storehouse man in the British Naval Base. At the end of every month, he handed his entire pay, in a brown envelope, to his wife. He left the entire running of the household to her, while he pursued his stage acting career and union activities. When Balji got older, the brown envelope was handed over to him.

"At a very early stage of my life, I had to handle my family finances," Balji says with a laugh that sounds like a cough. "And it was tough, because what my father gave was never enough to run the household. My mother had to find the rest, beg or borrow, and she did. She never allowed us to go hungry."

Balji leaves the relationship between his father and mother unsaid. I can tell that he is glad his own relationship with his wife is different. He ensures that she knows what he does and involves her in every way he can. His mother knew little of what his father did on stage and considered his stage career a "complete waste of time". On one occasion, when asked why she was so intent on educating both Balji and his younger brother, she replied sharply, "I want to get us out of this wretched life." There was a lot of pain and anger, she felt her husband was never interested in the running of the family, and she had to carry the family burden all on her own.

Does Balji have an image of his father that he is proud of? He was a trade union leader, and was responsible for a strike to get higher pay for the workers. It caused a lot of hardship for a lot of people, but Balji admired him for it. What his father did shaped his views, as a person who stood for the truth and fought for the underdog.

Aung San Suu Kyi is the youngest daughter of Aung San, who was the founder of the Myanmar Armed Forces and widely considered the Father of the Nation of modern-day Myanmar. He led the fight for independence from the British but was assassinated six months before Myanmar achieved that goal.[1] For his work towards Burmese independence and uniting the country, Aung San is revered as the architect of modern Burma and a national hero. Will his daughter meet a similar end? Even though she defended the military's handling of the Rohingya Muslims on a world stage, suspicions of her and her closeness to the image of her father will never be totally scrubbed from her persona.

Can we escape our past? Can we be totally new people from where we come from?

"There is a part of me that will always root for the underdog," says Balji. "And that's consciously or unconsciously influenced by my father, the union man. So, the apple doesn't fall far from the tree." He laughs. "But I don't think I want to replicate the nature of my parents' relationship with my wife, nor how they treated me with how I treat my children. That's why I wanted to move out, that's why I found Clover Way. It was to get a fresh start, to be who I wanted to be, how I wanted to raise my family."

It's noon now, and the humidity has reached an uncomfortable level. News of Myanmar blares out from the radio as Balji asks for the bill. In the next few months, the world would witness a Myanmar never seen before. From the very old to the very young, from the rich and wealthy to street urchins and the very poor, from celebrities to nobodies, in big cities and small townships, thousands upon thousands would take to the streets demonstrating their anger against the military and demanding a return to democracy and civilian rule.

My mind keeps going back to Balji's image of his mother waiting by the balcony … and how determined he was to change his life and own his new reality.

NOTES

1   Google Arts & Culture, "Aung San" <https://artsandculture.google.com/ entity/aung-san/m02sl5b?hl=en>.

Chapter 2

Friends and Relatives

In life, we can't choose our family, but we can choose our friends

Bad judge of character

Balji's fingers play with a teaspoon, a faraway gaze in his eyes. A light cool breeze flirts, whistling across our faces. We are enjoying an unusually windy February morning, right smack in the middle of the Lunar New Year. Today is *Renri*, which literally means "Human Day". It is the seventh day of the first month on the lunar calendar. In Chinese legends, Nuwa was the goddess who created the world, one animal each day. It started with the chicken, then dog, boar, sheep, cow, horse and, finally, human on the seventh day. From as early as the Han dynasty, it has been a tradition to celebrate everyone's "birthday" on the seventh day of the Chinese New Year.

"Should I wish you 'happy birthday'?" Balji laughs.

It has been an unusual Lunar New Year, to say the least. The co-chair of the Covid-19 task force, Lawrence Wong, had warned everyone to be prepared for a quieter, more subdued Chinese New Year. Only eight visitors are allowed at each household a day and the *lohei*, or the tossing of *yusheng*, should be done without the usual vocalisation of auspicious phrases. If one chooses to dine out, eight is also the limit and diners must remember to keep their face masks on during the tossing of *yusheng*. Reunion dinners with the extended family have not been possible as multiple table bookings are not allowed.

"This Chinese New Year has been just family, no friends," I take a sip of my *teh c*. "And I like it. It is so much better, less people, more time to talk. Thanks to COVID, I am finally enjoying Chinese New Year. No more unbearably loud *lohei*, no more big crowds. I remember the days when visiting meant squeezing with 20 or even 30 friends and relatives. I don't miss that at all."

Balji continues to play with his teaspoon, then lets out a laugh. "Family and friends, where do I start?" He stops, and then continues looking right into my eyes. "You can say I am a rather bad judge of character. Between family and friends, I have 'lost' a lot of money." He looks away and says, "Decades ago, but I remember each betrayal well."

I hold my breath. "What do you mean?" He must be exaggerating to make a point. Or is this a joke? There is not a lick of amusement on his face.

I must have stumbled onto a dark topic, and it is causing discomfort. We all have our fair share of bad friendships but betrayals or kinship or friendship gone wrong? Perhaps that's why he says so little about those who have cheated him.

"I have learned to listen to my inner voice now, trust my instincts," he says in a low, reflective voice. Then a forced smile appears on his face. "We don't listen or follow our instincts enough."

I look down. "Who betrayed your trust?"

Even though the wounds are decades old, the hurt is still not scrubbed from his heart, and this morning it resurfaces as a bruised smile. When he continues, his voice is dry and hollow. "When a stranger does something nasty, you don't think much of it," he shifts his gaze to the road. "But when it's someone closer to home, someone you have allowed into your family, or is part of your family, when that trust is compromised or broken, you take it very close to heart. You learn and you don't forget."

The stories come out slowly, between hums and haws. A bit like climbing a mountain, as he gets deeper into the stories, he is reaching higher up, the air is getting thin, and there is less air to breathe.

The exact date escapes him, it was in the 1970s. One morning, a relative turned up in his office and asked to see him urgently. "She told my secretary it was an emergency," the story begins, rather dramatically. "She needed $10,000, she said, to solve a life and death problem, otherwise she would commit suicide." Balji lets the drama hang in the air for a while. "While I half suspected she was putting up an act, I indulged her. Even though she was crying, she had the sense to accompany me home to fetch my POSB book," Balji's face continues to betray little. "She waited outside, didn't want to go inside the house in case she bumped into my wife." He never got his money back. "It was as if she was entitled to the money," he says, his voice dry as chalk.

There is resignation with little or no bitterness. I remember watching a documentary about wolves, and what the commentator said: "Wolves in the minds of most are evil; but they are also lonely and almost always hungry." Perhaps he sees those who betray him as wolves, they can't help themselves, and he just needs to stay far away from them.

Another story involves a close friend. When Balji launched his book, *Reluctant Editor*, those who attended the launch were surprised that the friend's name was not mentioned even once in the book. For someone who was once considered almost family, his silence spoke volumes.

"We became very close. He got to know my family, and I knew his father, wife and children. He needed money to start a food business." He had good business instincts and Balji was confident he would do well. The friend started a hawker stall and asked Balji for a loan of $40,000, promising to pay back in monthly instalments.

"I gave him the money," says Balji simply. "And he repaid up to $10,000 and then stopped," Balji laughs. "I found out later he also got into the property business. Many local Indians trusted him, and ended up losing their life savings. I was furious when I found that out."

"I am a bad judge of character. All these incidents taught me one iron rule: friendship or relationship cannot be built on money."

A father he never had

As we grow older, we keep in touch with fewer and fewer people. Those who stay in touch are "real" friends, or people who, for one reason or another, have become a part of our lives. Marlene Dietrich famously said: "It's the friends you can call up at 4am that matter."

Balji can count his real friends with the fingers on just one hand, with still a finger or two left uncounted. Friends you can count on are rare, like a full eclipse. But once in a while, you meet someone, and over time, the bond endures beyond friendship. When Balji first met Saleem, then a man in his early 30s and recently released from prison for drug offences, nothing pointed to any kind of bond, never mind friendship.

"He was suspicious," says Saleem. "I had submitted a piece to the letters page of *TODAY* on the Yellow Ribbon project, explaining why it didn't work. I got a call from Agatha Koh, the page editor, to come down to see them. There, I met Balji, who threatened to call the police. He thought what I had submitted wasn't written by me, that it was plagiarised." Saleem pauses, that afternoon in 2007 still vivid like a scenario that occurred just a day ago. "I got angry, I felt judged because of my background. But over half an hour, I managed to convince him that I wrote it."

"When I was shown the letter by the letters page editor, I was impressed," Balji's mind harks back to his days in *TODAY*. "The language was near perfect, the views articulated showed maturity. It was written by a thoughtful person. I was pleasantly surprised that it was written by someone with his background."

The meeting at *TODAY* lasted more than two hours; for Saleem, it was an important beginning of his writing being published. Saleem knew he had a talent for writing, but until then, only a few of his school teachers knew. "For someone with my past, to see my articles published not once, not twice, but on a regular basis, was more affirmative than anything the Yellow Ribbon project could do for me. What is more important, I knew Balji wasn't doing it out of pity, he got me to write because he saw my skill. The articles he got me to write were on important topics, requiring thorough research and cogent arguments. They acted as an outlet for me to express my thoughts, opinions and I took on various issues confronting us in society today. I raised awareness of issues that were pertinent to recovering drug abusers. It gave me confidence and a sense of purpose."

Currently, Saleem is the Head of Operations for a business with a social core to provide second chances for the disadvantaged who want to turn their lives around.

"This job suits me," Saleem says with easy calm in his voice. "I write a lot to ministries, MPs and statutory boards to help the vulnerable amongst us to get help, touching on areas like housing and financial assistance. Everyone needs a second chance, especially so for the disadvantaged in our society. This I know, first-hand. This is one way of paying it forward and it helps my own recovery as well." The calm that I sense is hard earned as he speaks candidly about working as a financial planner in a bank previously, and how difficult it was for someone with a record. "They can use it against you when it suits them," his voice weighs heavy with an uncomfortable memory.

"You lost your job because of it?" Although Saleem seems fine, I am not sure how far I should push.

"My relationships with my former employers were strained because of my past. When I lost my job, that was when I became most vulnerable." His youthful voice is excited and nervous at the same time. "That was when I got into depression and relapsed." He was caught and went back to prison, and this time, for seven years.

Through all the ups and downs, the one certainty he could count on was Balji's friendship.

"There were some things I couldn't even tell my wife, but I could be absolutely honest with Balji," he seems recharged. "He was, and still is, my sounding board. I find him to be down-to-earth, very accessible, even though he had a high profile with a powerful job. He is bold, insightful and always has a different perspective on things."

Would life have been different without knowing Balji?

Saleem is quiet, mulling over the question. "I see him regularly on Sundays for breakfast, in this restaurant called

Suriya at Tekka. With Covid it became tough, but we try our best to keep the date."

He hasn't answered my question.

"In life, we can't choose our family, but we can choose our friends," Saleem is getting around to the question. "Or if we are lucky, good friends choose us. I was lucky Balji chose me."

I sense there is more he wants to say.

"Balji is very observant, he has a keen eye for details." Saleem seems to be gravitating to a bigger point he is wrapping around his head. "I had an estranged relationship with my father, and even though we have reconciled, there were periods in the past when he was not a fatherly influence. Balji has been like a father I never had. But not just any father. He is always there, non-judgemental, always helpful. Both as a father and a friend."

The best kind.

Only the best food

Before I leave the apartment, I decide to check out Yoshi, the restaurant that businessman William Chua has booked for lunch. *Time Out*'s stark warning reminds me that we are still living in the midst of a pandemic:

Friendly warning! We're working hard to be accurate.
But these are unusual times, so please check that venues remain open.

Many fine-dining outlets have succumbed to the pandemic, so it's prudent to check. Peter Lim, the former editor-in-chief at SPH and Balji's boss, and William Chua are two of his oldest friends. The appointment is at 12.30pm. I arrive at 12.20pm and, to my surprise, both William and Peter are already seated. They look up and wave gingerly. With my mask and cap on, I can tell they are not entirely sure if they are greeting the right person.

"Balji, where are you?" William has Balji on the line. "We are all here waiting for you. For once, Peter is on time and you are late."

Balji's voice blares through the phone, now on speaker. "I'll be there in the next five minutes. Please start, don't wait for me."

"How William met Balji is an interesting story," says Peter. He looks at William from the corner of his eyes. "Tell the story, William."

"My wife and I used to be at the Jurong Country Club gym early, when there was no one around. And the only other couple there was Balji and his wife." William narrates his story slowly, and he seems to remember this particular one well. "In the 1990s, I think. When she wasn't looking, I liked sneaking up on Uma and checking the reading of the treadmill to see how fast she ran and how many calories she had burnt. He he he." William has a naturally loud, boyish snigger, the sort that comes from the gut and is unfiltered. "Did you say you are writing a book on Balji? What's it about?"

"Balji's story is ordinary in an extraordinary way," I begin, struggling to concentrate as my thoughts vacillate between taking in the Japanese restaurant and waiting for Balji. "Not many Singaporeans go through an arranged marriage in its most traditional sense, living through old, modern and contemporary Singapore as a journalist, and is now a sought-after observer and commentator of Singapore. Most people live, let live and get on. A small group like Balji try to make sense of the situation, to understand and hopefully contribute to improve on how we cope, how we live. Through him, I hope to tell a good Singapore story, of growing up in Singapore, working in Singapore and then, growing old in Singapore."

"It is not about his first book, right?" Peter asks.

"No."

"Good. When he was at SPH, he was a silent, quiet presence," Peter recollects. "He 'spoke' through actions, not words. If there was one leader who dared, it was him. There was an occasion at the *New Nation*," Peter begins. "Balji gathered a group of colleagues in *New Nation* and told them it was time to break through the notorious Straits Times Group's 'curtain of secrecy', around the so-called 'super bonuses'."

"Curtain of secrecy, super bonuses?" My curiosity is stirred.

Peter continues, "The lesser beings were paid contractual bonuses, the rates of which were known. The senior people and those who were exceptional performers that year were given extra bonuses. The rumour mill put top quantum at more than a year's salary! The identities of the super bonus recipients were understandably hidden."

"I see."

As he continues, the story seems to invigorate him, "Balji reportedly asked those at his meeting to declare their bonuses to each other and to pledge that they would continue to do so. It was a ballsy thing to do."

William Chua is smiling, an inside story from the doyen himself. Delicious.

"Management took that shocking development in their stride," says Peter, "but carried on with the policy of the secret 'supers'. One very senior editor in *The Straits Times* was heard lamenting about the 'troublesome people in *New Nation*

… why can't they behave like the ST folks and respect the company's culture', or words to that effect."

"Troublesome people in *New Nation*, ha ha ha." William signals to the chef who is waiting. "You can start the first dish," he says, looking at the entrance, expecting Balji any second. The first dish on our set menu is the seasonal starter, featuring a portion of *uni* atop a baby eggplant, pickled chrysanthemum and a little bit of *wasabi*, placed in a bowl of vinegar jelly. The *uni* melts in my mouth.

As Peter collects himself, his story finishes with a happy grin, and just then, Balji walks in. "I decided to take the bus," he seems a little breathless. "Didn't know which bus stop to get off at. I got off at the wrong one, a 15-minute walk away, my sincere apologies." His tone isn't apologetic and he is smiling. I half suspected he is late on purpose, so that I can get to know his friends better.

"Wah, this *uni* is good," Peter takes his time with the rich and creamy *uni* paired with all the other ingredients in the bowl. Something about people enjoying food makes me happy, which explains why I am such a big fan of good food programmes on TV.

"How long have you known each other?" I look at Peter and then Balji.

"For a long time, he was, of course, my boss," says Balji, still smiling. "When he left SPH in 1990, I felt more comfortable inviting him to my home. And Peter had a way with words, he told everyone the best Indian restaurant in Singapore was at 27 Clover Way. A clever way to get invited back."

"Come on, your wife *is* a good cook," there is tender warmth in Peter's voice. "And she knows what I like. When I visit, there is fish roe and everything else that I can't resist. The best Indian restaurant in Singapore for me. By the way, how are your relatives doing in India? The situation in India is nasty."

India has reported more than 200,000 deaths from Covid-19. The images coming out from India over the past few days are gut-wrenching. The country is like a war zone with scores of people dying outside hospitals, and family members desperately searching for oxygen cylinders for their loved ones.

"Things would have been different had the enemy's potential not been underestimated," says Balji in a steely voice.

I am sympathetic to Balji's view. Just a couple of months back, India had started to get back to normal. Instead of gearing up for the second wave, take lessons from countries that were already dealing with the next wave of infection, India, including its political leaders, were convinced that the deadly virus had left the country. While some claimed Indians had great immunity, others mocked Western countries for not being able to contain something as small as a virus. And Prime Minister Narendra Modi saw it as an opportunity to start his election campaign. In February, the Bharatiya Janata Party (BJP) passed a resolution which declared victory over Covid and hailed PM Modi as a "visionary". Between March and April, ahead of state elections, BJP held several mass rallies in the eastern West Bengal state with thousands in attendance.

"It is not that the second wave descended without any warning. The scientists and researchers had warned in September 2020 that the risk of a second wave was very real," anger simmers below the surface of Balji's words. "While all other countries went into war mode and planned strategies to combat the pandemic, Modi used the occasion to hold elections and campaigned in all the five states. His obsession to win the West Bengal assembly election was so acute that during the last two months, he addressed not fewer than 20 rallies. His lieutenant, Amit Shah, addressed nearly 30 rallies and held nearly two dozen road shows."

I know Balji misses his yearly visits to Kerala, and the pandemic has effectively put a stop to any visit this year. He goes on, not sparing Modi. "The first thing you learn from crisis management is that a crisis is the biggest test of leadership," Balji takes a page from our book on crisis management (see Chapter 4). "In handling the Covid pandemic, there was clearly a leadership deficit. Modi must go," he says, almost quietly. "He must take responsibility, little was done to build India's health infrastructure, he declared a false victory over the virus, celebrated the holy festival of *Kumbh* and went ahead with election rallies when the disease was spreading fast. He was focusing on political victory, not on the lives of his citizens."

The Indian Cabinet calls the pandemic a "once-in-a-century" crisis. A sense of anguish, hopelessness and anger has settled over the subcontinent. Normal life has come to a complete standstill, the mood is sombre all round with no one untouched by the crisis. Even privilege and connections have proved to be of little help as both rich and poor have struggled alike to get basic medical help, and many lives are being lost because of delays in getting it. There are now 18 million cases, each day adding some 400,000 to the toll.

"Wow, the beef is so good," Peter successfully brings the conversation back to the food. A few dishes have come and gone. For the main dish, we have a light *dashi* soup with Kagoshima Wagyu beef slices. The soup comes out piping hot, and Chef Yoshi immediately cooks the beef slices in the boiling soup. Before serving it, Chef Yoshi sprays water on the lid of the bowl. "Back in the day, each samurai would get a personal chef who would spray water on the pot lids before serving the dish," says the chef. "This is to ensure that no one has touched the dish before it reaches the samurai, preventing anyone from putting poison in the food." The simmering process has infused the soup with a savoury beef flavour.

"Very tender and juicy," says William. Unlike the rest of us, he is a regular at the restaurant, so when he says the food is good, it is good.

"Before you arrived, Peter told us about your days in *New Nation*," I want Balji to respond to what Peter started. "How you got the staff together to demand transparency."

"My memory is hazy," Balji's voice is tentative. "I had always felt that management kept details about bonuses secret so as to divide and rule the staff. The argument was that the staff will want their bonuses kept secret. I wanted to put that to the test. That was why I held the meeting with the *New Nation* team. The rest, well … Peter knows the management story and my story."

"Your solidarity with workers must have been instilled long ago by your father, a union man." I make an observation that Balji has brought up in his first book.

"Very much so," Balji's voice lifts.

Peter stands, looks at William and asks, "You know where the toilet is?"

"Let me walk you there, the way to the restroom is quite dark." William walks ahead. I remind myself that Peter, even though in the pink of health, is in his early 80s. And it moves me to see William, in his 60s, showing a gallant and protective side. All three men have grown old along with each other over the years. Their wives know each other.

"Both Peter and William flew to Canada for my daughter's wedding," Balji recalls with a touch of endearment in his tone. "We saw how each one of us became who we are. You cannot replace friends like these."

In the evening, I post on Facebook a picture of the four of us at Yoshi restaurant. "Rare meal with two of media's true veterans, Peter Lim and Balji Poravankara, with William Chua. And only the best food for best friends." I add three pictures of the food to illustrate what I mean by "the best food". Looking at the picture now, all four of us have grey or white hair, wear glasses and have known each other for at least two decades. Balji and Peter go way back (the following chapters will explore more of their experiences). The Facebook post is quickly "liked" by a host of people, with many comments.

"Some of our best journalists," writes Tommy Koh, our Ambassador-at-Large.

Bharathi Mohan: "Salutes to Peter Lim and Balji, the journalists I have worked with and admire to this day."

"The best brains who knew enough to not know enough," writes Kelven Tan.

Julie Lim: "Treasured veterans indeed. Hello to both, Peter and Balji."

"William Chua?" Irene Hoe asks. "The Goldbell guy?"

I use Facebook as a kind of diary – over the years, Facebook reminds me of what I have done, on this or that day, this month or that year. Today is important, I saw three friends who have grown older together, and the small telltale signs of real friendship. When one asked how the other was, he waited to hear the answer. One who walked ahead to make sure the path was clear and safe. And the entire afternoon, each one's presence was like a sheltering tree for the others.

So, we don't choose our family, God does that. We do choose our friends, or better still, our friends choose us. And like good wine, good friends get better with age. These are definitely friends who can call each other at four in the morning.

Author (standing) with Balji and his friends, William Chua (left) and Peter Lim (centre).

Chapter 3

Respect

The measure of any society is how it treats its women and girls

Living with three women

As a young boy, I used to get a hard-boiled egg for breakfast. I didn't think much about it until one day, my elder sister quietly asked if she could have half of my egg. I thought she was being greedy and replied, "Why must you have mine when you have your own?" She looked at me with wide-eyed surprise. "Only you get egg, we don't." I realised then, to my horror, that only my twin brother and I had eggs, my sisters never did.

When I was older, I understood why both my sisters didn't even finish primary school. They became domestic helpers so that the family had enough money, most of which went into paying school fees for my brother and I. My parents made no apologies for the way my sisters were treated. It was just the way sons were viewed as priorities while daughters came second in everything. Today, my sisters know the importance of education and make sure their own daughters don't suffer the fate they did. Things have changed over the years, it seems. Or have they?

As I approach from behind him, Balji's body heaves. As usual, his index finger plays with the rough table surface and his eyes are glazed, looking ahead at nothing in particular. He has something heavy on his mind this morning. Mama-san hovers, unsure if she should go ahead with our usual *kopi c kosong* and *teh c kosong*. I nod towards the counter where Gangsta Sista is stationed, she smiles with her eyes, visibly relieved. "I want to talk about Viswa, before we talk about anything else," he says. The grey 8.30am clouds hang low, promising an oppressively humid Monday morning.

Viswa Sadasivan was a former colleague in MediaCorp and we both know him reasonably well. He is a veteran presenter and talk show host, and also a former Nominated MP. He helmed a weekly online current affairs chat show, "Inconvenient Questions", a programme produced by his company, Strategic Moves Consultancy, in collaboration with the National University of Singapore Society (NUSS). The programme explored current Singapore topics and occasionally even hot, controversial political issues. Both Balji and I have been invited to appear on his show. On Thursday, 4 February 2021, around 3pm, just before the recording of a show on the status of women in Singapore, Viswa made a remark to an interviewee, stand-up comedian Sharul Channa. It was a remark that would turn his world upside down, one that he would remember for a very long time.

In a Facebook post later that day, Sharul said Viswa had made a sexual comment before the recording: he had asked why she was wearing a rose brooch, to which she replied: "I just put it on to distract from the pattern on my top." Then Viswa said: "It would be more distracting if you were wearing only that rose." After the interview, Sharul did not want the recorded interview aired and demanded an apology. She told *The Straits Times* that she had decided to post about the incident online because staying silent would have been against her principles.

"If I don't address it now, then I'm not being true to myself, I am not standing up for what I talked about during the interview," she said. "There's no point in someone treating me like this before the interview starts … when I know that the matter you are talking about is not honoured."

Sharul added that while it is permissible for her to crack jokes about herself, her body and her culture as part of her profession, she felt no one else had the right to pass sexual comments on her. "Even if I were in the prostitution business, and someone paid for my services, that person is not allowed to abuse or even belittle me," she said. Pointing to the government's designation of 2021 as the Year of Celebrating Singapore Women, Sharul said, "If we want to celebrate and bring awareness to equity for women, then a big part of it is to call out these problems. We should see sexual harassment in the form of words and comments. Even as small as comments, because that's where it all starts."

Viswa told *The Straits Times* he had written Sharul an email conveying "unconditional apology for causing hurt and for offending". He added that he could understand why she took offence. But he clarified, that to the best of his recollection, he had said: "It would have been more distracting if it was only the rose." He added that two female colleagues who were in the call told him in writing that they heard him say the same, and that he felt there was "absolutely no sexual innuendo intended" in what he had said. Viswa added that he has always stood for women's rights and spoken about this in various capacities.

Unfortunately for Viswa, Sharul was not alone. Doctoral researcher Kiran Kandade stepped forward when the issue erupted in social media, and then on mainstream media.

She told *The Sunday Times* that she had received sexually inappropriate text messages from Viswa five years back, in March 2016, while seeking consultancy and training work from him. And this time, there was a screenshot of a text message between them, where Viswa appeared to have asked Kiran if his "proposition to kiss passionately" had offended her. In a separate comment, Kiran added, "I have many more such texts and tales of encounter with him ... there's a lot more he said to me, to my face, when I went for meetings with him – how he'd like to kiss me, how he'd like to 'do things' to me," she wrote.

The Association of Women for Action and Research (AWARE) expressed support for both women. "These cases raise important points about women's experiences of workplace sexual harassment. It is not easy to speak up on the spot ... Often, the harassment happens quickly, and the recipient is taken aback, unsure about what they heard or so offended that they are at a loss for words."[1] AWARE added that the two women's experiences show how stressful and discomforting the "more subtle forms of workplace harassment can be" and how difficult it is to identify the type of harassment they are experiencing.

In a Facebook post, Viswa rejected AWARE's characterisation of his conduct as sexual harassment. He had already apologised adequately to both women, he asserted: to Kiran, via private email ("she needed to hear directly from me and not via social media"), and for Sharul, he had sent her a full statement of "unconditional apology" by email within minutes of finding out that she was upset. He also did not believe that an issue such as this could ever be resolved effectively on social media.

To this, AWARE responded: among other things, it said that "workplace sexual harassment is defined by the UN Convention on the Elimination of All Forms of Discrimination against Women as unwelcome sexually determined behaviour, physical contact and advances, sexually coloured remarks, showing pornography and sexual demand, whether by words or actions ... Such conduct can be humiliating and may constitute a health and safety problem ... it is discriminatory when the woman has reasonable grounds to believe that her objection would disadvantage her in connection with her employment, including recruitment or promotion, or when it creates a hostile working environment."

The organisation went on to stress how intent was "immaterial in establishing whether or not certain behaviour constitute harassment". AWARE noted that by the global standard definition of sexual harassment, "the determinant is, instead, whether the victim was offended or distressed by the statement and whether that response was reasonable. Intention can come into play but as a mitigating factor in deciding a perpetrator's punishment."

AWARE also addressed the role of social media in addressing cases of sexual harassment. AWARE noted that privately addressing allegations of harassment doesn't always work in the victim's favour as "entrenched systems are easily employed to silence, discredit and dismiss them", adding that private resolutions can be very "isolating" for victims. "Victims don't make the decision to go public on a whim," it stressed, adding, "We should not, therefore, be dismissive of social media as a channel for dialogue and justice, it is often the only recourse available." The organisation went on to point out that social media disclosures are also risky as it leaves victims open to victim-blaming and harassment, as evidenced by what Sharul and Kiran have had to face since going public with their stories.

All these culminated in the National University of Singapore discontinuing all projects with Viswa and his company, Strategic Moves. Viswa also stepped down as a member of the NUS Alumni Advisory Board.

The issue gripped Singapore, polarising public opinion. Many, mostly men and those who claim to know Viswa personally, think the case sets a dangerous precedent – men cannot be men anymore, they assert. The *#MeToo* movement which started in Hollywood in 2017 (with widespread sexual-abuse allegations against Harvey Weinstein, leading to high-profile firings, as well as criticism and backlash) should not be allowed to destroy political and corporate Singapore. On the opposite side, an equal number of women and men feel the Viswa scandal is a timely exposé of social and workplace harassment that has gone on for way too long. They feel that it is high time men know what women have to go through and that harassment and abuse of any kind must have consequences. Such public discourse, they feel, is healthy and will lead to eventual resolution of parity or equality between both sexes.

The episode has a disquieting effect on Balji, somehow it resonates personally with him. He wrestles with it – should he write a piece for Yahoo media? How can he add value to a topic that is raging on social media? How would it affect Viswa and, more significantly, Audrey, Viswa's wife?

"I know Audrey well; she is a good person. I don't want to add to her present anxiety," says Balji softly, almost as if to himself. "I look back at the years of living relatively freely, when guys could talk to a woman as if they were guys," he says, unfinished thoughts and arguments festering in his mind. "If a girl or woman knew you meant well, that it was part of the so-called locker room banter, as Trump put it, then it was alright. Women took it all within their stride, no one raised anything because it wasn't something that was done." It is clear he has been thinking hard about the issue. "What most Singaporean men fail to realise is that times have changed. When Lee Kuan Yew decided to educate women, bring them into the workforce, it started something that cannot be reversed. What this shows is that women have changed, but it is also clear that men haven't, at least some men."

Balji brings up something else, a fact that explains why the issue is almost personal to him. "I live with and am completely engrossed with the lives of three women, my wife and two daughters. When women are also seen in their roles as mothers, sisters, wives and daughters, then it is almost impossible not to treat women with respect." He lets out a sigh. "I may sound old-fashioned, but respecting women is something important to uphold in my life."

I recall what Michelle Obama said about women and society: "The measure of any society is how it treats its women and girls."

"Absolutely," Balji says in resounding agreement.

Change started in the West. Turning the clock back to the 1960s, it wasn't just the civil rights movement that was at a fever pitch in the US, it was also the rights of women, many of whom found their voices in a song. It was probably the most stirring anthem for the feminist movement, but "Respect" – the inspiring song that crowned Aretha Franklin as the Queen of Soul – was written by a man, begging for a break from his wife.[2]

1967, Atlantic Records Studio, New York. It was Valentine's Day; an almost unknown 24-year-old gospel singer sat down at a piano and recorded "Respect", a song written and first recorded by Otis Redding. Aretha Franklin did not know it then, but the song would become an anthem for the civil rights movement, and more importantly, the women's movement.[3]

Soulful, revolutionary, unapologetic, unflinching, it was almost a declaration of independence, "Respect" became a soundtrack for the 1960s.[4] A song originally written by a man had ironically become an uncompromising call for women demanding society in general and men in particular to regard them differently. The standout part of the song was the use of backup female singers and the song's most famous lines, boldly spelled out:

R-E-S-P-E-C-T –
Find out what it means to me.

Released in April 1967, it soared to number one on the charts and stayed there for 12 weeks, winning Franklin two Grammy awards that year. It was a pivotal time in the feminist and civil rights movements, and Franklin's version of the song became emblematic of both. When she recorded the song, it wasn't in an attempt to make it a political anthem, it was personal. "You are going to give me respect when you come home" – the lyrics as changed by Franklin.[5]

Franklin passed away in 2018 at the age of 76. In an interview, she had expressed her belief that the song would be relevant for a long time, "as long as there is a lot of disrespect."

That was in the 1960s, it's now 2022. Franklin was right. Times may have changed, men and women have moved on, yet things have essentially remained the same. Women like Sharul and Kiran need organisations like AWARE to police, protect and defend them. In India, a country Balji is intimately familiar with, one rape is reported every 15 minutes. The country is still run by men, despite having had a female prime minister. Beyond India, in many countries, a woman is still an object, still perceived as "something" rather than "someone". "Respect" might have stayed in the charts for 12 weeks, but did it change anything? When I listen to Franklin's blistering rendition, when I read and re-read the version of events given by Sharul and Kiran, I begin to understand the unease in Balji, and why, living with three women in his life, he takes this issue of respect personally. In some homes, the boy still gets the egg while the girl just looks on.

Mothers

"I was the first son after five girls, you can imagine the joy of my parents, especially my mother. I was treated like a prince. My mother fed me the best food money could buy, I had mutton almost every other day," a lean and health-conscious Balji looks back on his early years. "I became obese and my mother was proud of it. Being fat showed everyone she loved me and took good care of me."

Food was just a symptom of the problem. Deeper, underneath what he was given and fed, was the attitude towards women.

"When you are doted on, when you can have anything you want while you see that your sisters don't enjoy the same privileges, you assume or begin to acquire the attitude that the opposite sex isn't your equal, that maybe, they are even beneath you." Balji has a difficult love-hate relationship with his mother. While he does not refer directly to her, I sense the reference to her in almost all his remarks made about mothers. "So, over time, you become less sensitive. And that's when you abuse them, put them in their place when they don't behave the way you want them to. I put the blame on mothers, at least traditional mothers. And believe me, there are many traditional mothers around even in the developed world."

Most of us think of ourselves as modern, that old or traditional notions of women are not part of our outlook and mental makeup. However, as reported in an online BBC News article, "a new UN report has found almost 90 per cent of men and women hold some sort of bias against females":[6]

The "Gender Social Norms" index analysed biases in areas such as politics and education in 75 countries.

Globally, close to 50 per cent of men said they had more right to a job than women. Almost a third of respondents thought it was acceptable for men to hit their partners. There are no countries in the world with gender equality, the study found.

The article highlights examples set out in the report:[7]

Zimbabwe had the highest amount of bias with only 0.27 per cent of people reporting no gender bias at all. ...

In Zimbabwe, 96 per cent of people expressed a bias against women's physical integrity – a measure covering support for violence against women and opposition to reproductive rights. In the Philippines, 91 per cent of people held views that were detrimental to women's physical integrity.

In terms of women in political roles, the report found that "about half of the world's men and women feel that men make better political leaders" (55 per cent in China and 39 per cent in the US). The article continues:[8]

> Pedro Conceição, head of UNDP's Human Development Report Office said: "We have come a long way in recent decades to ensure that women have the same access to life's basic needs as men.
>
> "But gender gaps are still all too obvious in other areas, particularly those that challenge power relations and are most influential in actually achieving true equality. Today, the fight about gender equality is a story of bias and prejudices."

In economic terms, it was also found that "women are paid less than men and are much less likely to be in senior positions. Globally, 40 per cent of people thought men made better business executives."

This is also evident in the gender preference of boys over girls practised worldwide, resulting in an imbalanced gender ratio, as discussed in an NPR article:[9]

> Nature favours boys at birth, with a consistent worldwide gender ratio of about 105–107 males born for every 100 females. But females eventually catch up. ... In developed countries, like the U.S., the U.K., and Canada, women begin outnumbering men at about age 55.
>
> So in the natural course of things, the male advantage in numbers decreases over a lifetime, with women ultimately gaining the advantage in numbers.

But in some countries the balance is tipped unnaturally toward an overabundance of boys, an imbalance that is likely to last through the reproductive years.

The article explains:

In 1995, only six countries had such a marked imbalance of boys to girls. Today, 21 countries have a skewed sex ratio favouring boys.

It states that "several things have combined to lead to what researchers call 'missing women'." In pointing out that "technology has enabled even the poorest of countries to bypass the natural gender balance", the article refers to an interview with Professor Valerie Hudson of Texas A&M University:[10]

Abortions of females can happen before anyone in the community notices a pregnancy, she says. And when girls are abandoned or neglected so severely that they die, it often doesn't create much of a stir among people who understand the preference for boys. "No one raises it as a public issue within the community, so while it's not secret, it isn't commented upon," says Hudson.

The article presents this stark reality:[11]

The result of sex-selective abortions, infanticide and neglect of baby girls, according to the United Nations Population Fund, is more than 117 million "missing" females in Asia alone, and many more around the world.

Why these statistics? They are hard facts or truths, and although our families and friends may not resort to extreme

1

physical measures, the subtle day-to-day preference for boys over girls have behavioural consequences with lasting societal effects.

"Modern Asia is still governed by some ancient practices, tradition is alive and well, and these include some pretty disgusting customs about gender," says Balji, his eyes rise for that dramatic effect. But Balji's temperament and emotional makeup goes against the typical Indian or Asian male macho stereotype. It might have been his father's influence, a stage actor and a unionist, fighting for the underdog. Balji appreciated the sensitive way his father treated his mother, and how his sisters were treated. But, ultimately, it was his wife and her way of running the household that shaped his approach and regard for women.

"As a journalist, I am curious about human beings and their actions, male and female. I get to know and write about extraordinary women," he waves his right hand to anchor his point. "But I must say, I learned a lot more from my wife. When you appreciate a human being for being a good person, one who is hardworking, always kind and considerate, it doesn't matter if the person is a man or woman. Of course, my wife is a woman, and I will look out for her and protect her in areas where women are generally weaker. But she is first and foremost my partner in life, a person I consult with in all major decisions. And in our journey as husband and wife, I have learned so much, cheered on by her personal development and transformation."

From the very start, on the night of their wedding itself, he had a strong intuition that the woman he married would be a capable wife. He allowed her almost complete independence, and when he saw how that empowered and developed her, he became convinced that women should be allowed total latitude to be their full selves and achieve their full potential. And to extend that one further, wherever possible, to be exposed to the best education. To this end, husband and wife decided that it was important that they send both their daughters abroad, one to the UK and the other to Canada. "Not just to further their studies but to expose them to other ways of life, other cultures." Once again, Balji has that faraway look. "There is always the risk of them not coming back, but we feel it is important for them to be exposed to the ways of the world." And when his second daughter decided to stay in Toronto having met her boyfriend there, Uma and Balji were fine with it; it came with the territory.

Outside of his household, the person who has a direct impact on his attitude towards women is his former boss, the gentlemanly Peter Lim. Peter has a reputation of being a lady's man, in the most charming and positive way possible. For Peter, women are deserving of special reverence, not because of their weaknesses but because of their strengths — the moral and spiritual constitution of women, as opposed to the physical, showy prowess of men. Men flex their muscles and make a show of being the breadwinner of the household, but women are the ones who hold up the complex institution of family together.

Peter converted his apartment in Tiong Bahru into a medical ward when his mother became bedridden, against the advice of his friends and colleagues who thought it was unnecessary, as there were cheaper and more "sensible" alternatives. For Peter, he wanted the best for his mother; expenses were not spared, with two nurses rotating to provide her with round-the-clock care for two years.

"Men's complex relationship with women can be traced back to how they were brought up by their mothers," says Balji with a straight face. "Peter Lim's protective love for his mother has a back story. He found out that his late father had another family during his father's funeral, when another woman turned up with children in tow. Can you imagine how his mother must have felt? Peter decided then that he would never marry, as he knew deep down he wasn't a one-woman man, and he would not subject any woman to the brutal, humiliating 'secret' his mother had to endure."

He adds, "How men treat woman begin when they are children. When mothers treat all their children as equals, it is a very good start."

For both his daughters, Deepa and Divya, their source of confidence and assurance comes not just from their mother, but more importantly from their father, and observing how he regarded and treated women as they were growing up.

"I saw how much respect my father accorded women in general," says Deepa. "As an adult, I had many women who worked in the newsroom who'd tell me, 'Your father is the kindest boss I had when I was pregnant. He let me work from home and saved my pregnancy.' This came from many women reporters I got to know."

"I don't think I ever thought of myself being his 'daughter'," says Divya. "Just his child. There was never a discussion about gender from the perspective of how he thought girls or women should behave. It was always about respecting people and being a good person."

At work, but more importantly, at home.

"His behaviour was the same way with my mum," Divya continues. "He gave her space and room to grow, to do what she wanted to do. He didn't interfere and gave his opinion when he was asked … This was the same way he treated my sister and me. Any profession we chose, he and my mom supported it. When we asked for advice, he was there to lean in."

And how he treated his wife assured them.

"We saw how much space he gave my mom, the encouragement, the voracious volumes of books and news she read. A lesser man would have been threatened, but instead, she blossomed as a self-taught investment guru, an important source of information for the entire family. My father is the reason I have chosen to marry Sri … They are mirror images."

Independence is something his daughters treasure, yet when needed, he was and is never far. There was one episode Divya will never forget: "It was during the SARS outbreak and my ticket had been originally booked to fly to Singapore from Toronto via Hong Kong. Of course, we had to change that flight and my dad suggested I fly back home with a stopover in France instead. He knew I was nervous about travelling during the outbreak, so he decided to meet me in

The three women in Balji's life.

Paris and we spent a few days in the city, and then in the south of France. We did a lot of sightseeing, a lot of eating, some hiking in the Pyrenees and a lot of talking. Not sure how many daughters get a one-on-one trip like that with their dad and it is something I'll never forget."

Someone once told me, a woman wants a man to protect her like a daughter, love her like a wife, and respect her like a mother. Ultimately, it is respect for the opposite sex, and this needs to be inculcated right from the start, when the men are still boys.

ENDNOTES

1   <https://twitter.com/awarenews/status/1358326224951513088>.

2   Fiachra Gibbons and Anthony Lucas, "How Aretha Franklin made 'Respect' a feminist anthem", Agence France-Presse, 16 August 2018 <https://au.news.yahoo.com/aretha-franklin-made-respect-feminist-anthem-143229882--spt.html>.

3   DeNeen L Brown, "How Aretha Franklin's 'Respect' became an anthem for civil rights and feminism", *The Washington Post*, 16 August 2018 <https://www.washingtonpost.com/news/retropolis/wp/2018/08/14/how-aretha-franklins-respect-became-an-anthem-for-civil-rights-and-feminism/>.

4   See note 2.

5   See note 2.

6   BBC News, "Gender study finds 90% of people are biased against women", 5 March 2020 <https://www.bbc.com/news/world-51751915>.

7   See note 5.

8   See note 5.

9   Susan Brink, "Selecting Boys Over Girls Is A Trend In More And More Countries", NPR, 26 August 2015 <https://www.npr.org/sections/goatsandsoda/2015/08/26/434616512/selecting-boys-over-girls-is-a-trend-in-more-and-more-countries>.

10 See note 8.

11 See note 8.

Chapter 4

Second Act

A new kind of independence

Retire to work

"I am in my 70s," says Balji, inhaling deeply and holding his breath briefly, before letting it out slowly, almost like a declaration of independence. "I am a grandfather now, with different responsibilities. I have financial independence; I engage in projects that interest me. It is a new kind of freedom, if you like. While I enjoy this lifestyle, I am also learning how to handle and manage it every single day."

Balji has guarded his independence jealously. "True, there is no such thing as total independence, we need to work with people around us," he strikes a pensive note. "We know real independence when we are granted it, and it is important. Independence is a critical proviso for creative endeavour. You need it to be who you really are. You need to be bold enough to say, 'This is how I feel.'"

It is this precious independence that led to his "early retirement".

Balji thought about retirement way before he reached the age where he needed to, in his early 50s. It was triggered by an incident that happened to his boss and best friend, the chief editor of *The Straits Times*, Peter Lim. He had a ringside seat observing how Peter Lim tried to run the newsroom with some degree of independence and paid the price for it by having to resign. Peter was in his early 50s when a board member told him, "Your deputy is ready to take over." (In a plane ride from Yangon to Singapore, then Prime Minister Goh Chok Tong told Cheong Yip Seng that he would be taking over as Chief Editor.)

"When I heard this, a chill ran down my spine," says Balji, when I ask him about the incident that got him thinking seriously about retirement. "By standing firm on what you believe in, you could be faulted because it wasn't in step with the thinking of the powers that be. Peter took it within his stride, he went on to launch *The New Paper* and did other things for SPH. I wouldn't be able to do what he did after being treated like that."

"So, you retired early?"

"Before anyone could tell me that my deputy was ready to take over, I removed myself from that very possibility. When a person is in his 50s, he is at the prime of his life. It is that age where his experience is finally sufficient for him to be considered for the top jobs. But, most importantly, he is at the point in his life where his life's passage can impart the wisdom that youth cannot. And in the political and corporate world, good judgements are often instructed and informed from wisdom. Put simply, some grey hair or no hair is not necessarily a bad thing."

If one thinks of Joe Biden and Donald Trump, then someone in his 50s is actually young. When they were in their 50s, Biden and Trump were only amassing and gathering the requisite experiences they would eventually need to lead the most powerful country in the world. They became presidents only in their 70s. A study published in the *New England Journal of Medicine* in 2018 found that the best and most productive years of one's life are between 60 and 80 years. A person reaches the top of his or her potential at age 60 and this continues into his or her 80s.

By retiring officially from the corporate world in his early 50s, Balji took back real control of his life. At the same time, he had seen what it takes to appease corporate Singapore. Very often, people who own or have the ultimate say know little of the businesses they control. In Singapore, especially in government organisations and statutory boards, selected men and women in top jobs are rotated, given stints in a variety of fields. They have broad experiences but little depth in any of the fields. Managing them, or "managing up", is a full-time job. It takes away the precious time necessary for real, creative work.

"I retired in my mid 50s to have the independence to be my own man," he says with quiet force. But it wasn't necessarily the most popular thing to do, even within his family. "It meant quitting at the apex of my career. The peak. And, of course, not many people understand this. They ask why, what happened? People expect you to carry on when you are doing well. It is not common to 'retire' when you are at the top of your game."

But when we take out the word "retire", the landscape changes. In some countries, the concept of retirement doesn't even exist.

In Okinawa, men and women live an average of seven years longer than any other people or race in the world and have one of the longest disability-free life expectancies. They also have an outlook on life that is very different from the rest of the world. While we think of retirement as the golden age of golf greens, recreational hobbies and taking care of grandchildren, they don't even have a word for it. Literally nothing in their language describes the concept of stopping work completely. Instead, they have the word *ikigai*, which translates roughly into "the reason you wake up in the morning".

And everyone has a reason to wake up in the morning, a reason for living … everyone has an *ikigai*. And this is the secret to long life and happiness. This reason for living is what keeps them always busy, what allows them to remain active, what they enjoy doing, what their real purpose in life is.

Last year, I finished the book, *Soul of Ink*,[1] on 100-year-old artist Lim Tze Peng. Although he was an artist since his teens, he was also a teacher and principal. He retired at 60 to become an artist full time. In his 80s, he conceived a way of writing calligraphy that cannot be read. He called it muddled calligraphy, or *hutuzi*. To him, calligraphy should be appreciated as painting, not something to make sense of. The local calligraphic establishment was up in arms, rubbishing it as heresy. It was only when the mainland Chinese gave it the thumbs up that local public opinion slowly changed. Today, *hutuzi* is not only celebrated but also seen as an artistic way of approaching calligraphy. Lim Tze Peng was awarded the Cultural Medallion in his 80s, and the very rare and prestigious Meritorious Award in his mid 90s.

Still painting, he said this on his 100th birthday: "Give me a few more years, I can contribute more." Asked about retirement, he laughed. "The Chinese word for retirement is to retreat permanently. The image one has is to disappear from the scene. For me, it is the opposite. I consider my advanced years as the golden years of my life. I no longer have to fuss with the mundane, I have taken care of those, now I truly live." Although he does not know the concept of *ikigai*, he is a living example of it. Every morning, he cannot wait to be in his studio to put on the rice paper what he sees in his mind. His secret to a long life: "Art is my oxygen; it keeps me alive. When you have a true passion, when you can't wait to wake up every morning to do it, it will sustain you and keep you 'young' and occupied." And the artist does not mean "just painting" to keep him occupied. At 100, he seeks "breakthroughs", which means new advancements in his knowledge or technique in art. "I am experimenting all the time, pushing the boundaries, pushing myself. When I am able to ambush or surprise myself, that's when I am happiest!"

What is Balji's "second act"? Would he, like Lim Tze Peng, find his true calling after the so-called "retirement"?

Second act

The dictionary defines "second act" to mean something a person devotes his time to "later in life", after retiring or quitting his original occupation. There is no mention that one's second act can actually be better than one's first. Peter Drucker, the father of modern management, who died in 2005 at the age of 95, is a role model for a "better" second act. Drucker had a long career as a writer, professor, consultant and self-described "social ecologist" and his second act radiated purpose and meaning. Most of Drucker's 39 books were published after his 65th birthday.

Notably, according to Drucker, one's second act should be a looser, less structured lease of years where one's passion rules paramount. Ideally, it is a happy combination of talent and passion. Some of Drucker's tips: "Doing something you love is a great business plan. Next, try to break new ground, there is no age limit to starting up. Even while you are doing something you love, allow yourself to learn new things about what you love."

A second act, therefore, can allow a person to go into areas the "first act" couldn't. With knowledge, wisdom and experience, and most important of all, a new freedom, a person's second act can unleash a life-altering lease of many years, allowing the person to actually fulfill his life aspirations.

When Balji stepped out of MediaCorp's *TODAY* in 2003, he was only in his mid 50s. "It was a new feeling, retiring early from a structured big company," Balji remembers the day almost 20 years ago. "I didn't feel old, I didn't feel tired. I was liberated in a way I didn't understand then, but looking at it now, it was energising." He stops, his face wearing a hidden smile. "People always ask me, 'Do you miss the newsroom? Do you miss the chase?' Honestly, no. Retiring from MediaCorp, instead of shrinking my options, actually expanded my horizon."

What was on this mind? "I consciously set out to do something that combined my experiences but also what I knew I could do but never did," he quietly asserts. "And that was putting creative ideas behind products. It is media still, but we are not selling newspapers or the news, but using my understanding of the media to help clients sell products."

Crush was a group of young professionals who wanted to make a difference in the advertising space. When they found out that Balji had left *TODAY*, they approached him to start a public relations arm for the group, and that was how Bang was born.

"My specialty was government clients, given my history of working with ministries and statutory boards," he says, folding his arms. "I started the company the same year I left *TODAY* and … it was two very exciting years in PR. Our unique calling card was, 'Don't just get published, get read'. Clients were happy when they got covered by the media. I went one step further, I wanted to ensure that what was published was read too. And clients saw the crucial difference."

An example. The client was the National Environment Agency (NEA), and the account was on how waste was managed. "As I said, I didn't just want coverage, I also wanted the coverage to be read. I went for something dramatic, something that shocked, something that people would want to know more about, which meant they would want to read about it." The island Pulau Semakau was where waste was treated and reused. Instead of just looking at the facilities and showing photographs of machines, he convinced the client to go for a never-before-seen aerial shot. "I managed to convince the client to hire a helicopter with a photographer. It wasn't in the budget but I persuaded them to do it anyway, to get an aerial view of the island, an angle not seen before." The photograph turned out to be a stunner, a breathtaking overview of the island. It made page one of *The Straits Times*, it was the sort of media mileage money couldn't buy. More importantly, it was also the sort of story people were intrigued enough to want to read about."

Another milestone was an unusual stint with the *New Straits Times* in Malaysia. Balji's task was to convert a broadsheet into a compact paper, a bit like turning *The Straits Times* into *TODAY*. "As project head, the work was demanding but not undoable," he remembers. "My problem was resistance from the middle-level people. Most of the senior staff didn't understand why a Singaporean was hired, instead of a local Malaysian. Since the senior staff had a lot of say in the day-to-day decisions, every decision I made was either blocked or delayed because there was no green light given. They made it clear they were not cooperating with me."

Balji's strength had always been his special bond with rank and file, not top or senior management. And he found a "secret weapon" in a lady reporter. "She had a fantastic scoop," he recalls with relish. "She was doing a story on prisoners and their last meals, or literally, their "last supper". I immediately thought of a visual spread of what they ate because no one had seen what prisoners on death row ate. We planned and found out in detail what each dish was, bought the ingredients and replicated the meal in the way that they would eat them … their last supper. I still remember one tray was left empty because one of the guys on death row refused to eat. It was, quite simply, high drama."

The result was an extraordinary spread of unique pictures: food for those on death row. "The subject matter was unusual, almost forbidden. People were intrigued and interested in the pictures, and the way we laid them out delivered a knockout punch. The impact was great – everyone noticed and gasped."

The middle-level staff sat up following the success of the story. The lady reporter became his "ambassador" to the senior management, and the rest of the project with the *New Straits Times* proceeded smoothly.

In late 2005, the CEO of *The Hindustan Times* invited Balji to New Delhi to produce a "down-market" paper. He was not convinced of the strategy and made a study of the market in India himself. Instead of a paper pitched to the low end of the reading demographic, he counter-proposed, advising the CEO to start a paper for women.

"My idea was not a paper on how to dress, how to be successful on a date, but a newspaper that would treat and respect women as another section of the readership." For example, what they thought of the prevailing government policies, women's views on political and economic issues, not just social issues. "In other words, open it up to the potential of the vast women's market in India."

After working on the concept for weeks with an Indian journalist and an Indian artist, Balji was ready to present his prototype to the management. "The CEO asked the lady boss of the company to sit in. She in turn asked two of her sons to join the panel," says Balji, with a laugh in his voice. "It ended with the woman asking both her sons what they thought and would they read the paper? They both said they liked the paper because by reading the paper, they would know how women thought and behaved."

At the beginning of 2015, I was invited by RHT Law Taylor Wessing to consider starting a media arm for their law firm. It was a revolutionary idea for a law firm. The proposition was: the lawyers would help their clients win in the court of law; we, the media arm, would continue the crucial journey for the clients, helping them win in the court of public opinion. A studio, complete with state-of-the-art cameras and lighting was built for us right in the middle of downtown Shenton Way. And so, RHT Digital & Media was conceived. It was the first time I found myself wearing a media hat in a legal environment. Somehow, I was confident, because I had Balji in my team as consultant.

Over the years, we landed big clients like BreadTalk and UOB because they knew ours was a team with media veterans. Particularly noteworthy was the weekly column

Balji contributed to the company, "Wednesdays with Balji". Every Wednesday, top management from the law firm looked forward to the column; it was well read, shared and used for their work. "We hit a century," Balji remembers, when the column chalked up 100 editions over a period of more than two years. Our time and experiences at RHT Digital & Media culminated in our crisis management book, *We Have a Problem: Crisis and Reputation Management in the Digital Age.*[2] The book was co-authored by Balji, lawyer Eugene Quah, digital guru Keith Nakamura and myself.

Perhaps the closest Balji got to "participating" in the political stage in Singapore was the 2017 Presidential Election. That presidential election was reserved for Malay candidates, and the founding chairman and CEO of Second Chance Properties Ltd, Mohamed Salleh Marican, declared his interest to contest. Balji and I were asked to spearhead the media team, to prepare him and his team for the gruelling campaigning which awaited them.

Salleh Marican believed he could be president, although Second Chance Properties' shareholder equity was only between $254.3 million and $263.25 million in the past three financial years, which fell short of the $500 million required for automatic qualification as a candidate. He felt he could convince the Presidential Elections Committee to qualify him, as long as they were satisfied that he had the experience and ability to effectively carry out the functions and duties of the Office of the President.

Balji's decades of media experience came in handy, as the team quickly realised that every move, however small and seemingly insignificant, was under the intense scrutiny of the media. Every post on Facebook or Instagram was carefully considered; every trip out of the house, even to the office, could be a strategic move or a PR trap. Salleh's flashy car was quietly hidden and his attire (and that of his wife's) went through a TV-friendly "correction". Balji's counsel of when and what to say became the biblical guide. The presidential candidate was coached every day and by the time he collected his application form in June, he was media ready and all set to give the other two candidates, Speaker of Parliament, Halimah Yacob, and chairman of Bourbon Offshore Asia, Farid Khan, a run for their money.

"I seriously thought he had a fighting chance," Balji says, looking back at the fateful election. "The majority of Singaporeans prefer their president to be apolitical and Salleh represented that. Of the three, he was the most 'Malay', and the community looked up to him as a leader, his being the first Malay company to be listed, and he was a shining example of a family man. He would have been a good president."

On 11 September 2017, the Presidential Elections Committee rejected his application, issuing only one Certificate of Eligibility to Halimah Yacob.

A new world

The day after Balji walked out of the *TODAY* newsroom, Arrian cried himself into the world. And quite suddenly, Balji became a grandfather. Looking into a glorious sunset, he remembers telling himself that not all endings need to be bad. Endings can spell the end of one thing and the beginning of something else. The beauty of a sunset is that, not long after, there will be a sunrise, like Arrian's birth.

"Growing up, my parents rarely showed outward signs of affection, though Divya and I knew we were loved," says

Deepa with a grin. "In 2008, when Arrian was born, that changed. Both my parents had different stirrings, I believe. My mother felt stirrings of finally having a son. She wanted boys her whole time as a mother and that year, the universe gave her a grandson. She doted on him, bought him the best toys and laced his cheeks with kisses all the time till I got jealous!"

For Balji, it presented, for the first time, a chance to "parent" full time.

"When my daughters were growing up," Balji casts his mind back to the newsroom, "I was in the thick of my corporate career. How they were being brought up was important, but I had a full-time job. And full time for a journalist or editor, was *full time*. Late nights were normal, but it was the constant reading up, thinking and observing, and to be ahead of the news and current affairs that took up most of my time."

Being out of a full-time job meant he could devote time to being a grandfather. "I had thought a lot about being a grandfather when Deepa was pregnant, how I should go about being one. I am very conscious that I am different from my wife, who has no problem with showing her feelings and expressing her love for the grandchildren. I have difficulty doing that, showing my love for someone in public, and I can't be a different person just because I am older."

While parents are crucial in the upbringing of their children, the role of grandparents can be equally important. "I felt, and still feel, that a grandparent's role is a complementary one. I cannot be a substitute for their parents, or go against what they wish. But that doesn't mean I can be irresponsible and spoil them too. My wife and I love our grandchildren, but we cannot be unthinking, completely emotional and just let them run all over us."

Deepa and Sri do not indulge in "baby talk" with their children, as Balji noticed from the start. "They talk to their boys, however young, almost as they would to an adult. The choice of words may be simpler, but there is no gushing or over-expression to appease. Also, the English used is always proper, spoken in full sentences." And this is also the tone the grandparents take, aligning with and supplementing the parents, and not confusing the grandchildren.

Arrian was an unusually naughty child who didn't like to attend kindergarten and had a view of every single teacher. "I remember taking him to Peirce Reservoir in the mornings, my way of cooling him down before going to the kindergarten. I was obsessed with finding a way to get through to him, to make him less restless."

By involving himself in his grandson's everyday life, whether it is taking him to school, sports practices, music lessons or taking him along when he runs errands, Balji gets into his grandson's world. He questions his grandson often and allows himself to be questioned. Most importantly, he listens to his grandson.

"Arrian takes Malay classes," Balji leans back, eyes focused. "I speak to him in Malay, suggest different words to use, check his spelling. Sometimes I even discuss politics with him. I know he is young, only a boy. I am not sure how much he understands, but it doesn't matter. As long as he is attentive, I will continue."

From an almost uncontrollable kid at four, Arrian at 13 today is mature beyond his years. "His parents were patient, and with their love and with my wife's patience, he has become a loving young man. We are all proud of him. Just today, going to the market, Arrian voiced a concern," says

Balji, with warmth in his voice. "When the Covid situation is over, when you both decide to travel again, be careful," he speaks in his grandson's voice. "The planes have not flown for a long time, you cannot be sure that they are safe, the engines of the plane may not be good." Of course, Balji knows SIA has already started flying and the planes have all been tested, but he decided not to dampen the boy's initiative and care.

"I told him, 'I'll be careful.'"

This new grandfather-grandson relationship is the result of a rough patch Balji went through with Arrian, one that he chronicled in his contribution to the book, *Letter to My Son*,[3] a compilation of various letters from fathers to their sons, except for Balji, his was a letter to his grandson:

> Let me start with an apology. And it is an unreserved one, with no caveats, no ifs and buts. I apologise for being tough and rough with you when you were growing up. If I had understood how you were emotionally affected by my behaviour, I would have been more understanding and accepting of your boisterous, restless and rebellious nature. So, here it is: Sorry.
>
> I should have learned from the way your grandmother dealt with you. She loved you with no inhibitions. I could see it was true love. The kind of love many men hardly display in their interactions with their children and grandchildren. Some call it the yin-yang relationship where one takes the soft approach and the other, hard.
>
> A quick back story is needed. About six years ago, when you were about five, I used to fly off the handle

because of your behaviour. There were few occasions when I raised my hand when I saw you doing things which I felt were inappropriate …

One day, your father shocked me with these words: "Arrian told me that you don't love him." Those words were painful to hear. Which grandfather doesn't love his grandson? I could hardly sleep that night …

I began to focus on your good qualities. As I began to watch you closely, I realised you liked things technical. You knew the mobile phone inside out; you knew nearly every part of my car, even teaching me how to use the park assist mechanism …

… our relationship began to change. I hope you have noticed that. You have become more caring, advising me to wash my hands with soap regularly because of the havoc Covid-19 is inflicting on the world. I was very touched when one night, you came into my bedroom to check if I were breathing.

You are also becoming disciplined and responsible. You finish your homework on time and without any prompting, pull up your younger brother when he steps out of line. And you have become a straight shooter, once even telling off your teacher for screaming and walking out of class …

The transformation has been admirable. There are still some rough edges but I am convinced you will iron them out in no time …

I grew up in a different time, a different world. Times were tough with nobody giving this minute dot called Singapore a chance to survive. The government under Lee Kuan Yew and its citizens pulled together and we have this man-made marvel before us. I belonged to the lucky generation. As Singapore progressed, the people of my generation benefitted ... The government forced a saving culture on us by mandating that our Central Provident Fund had sufficient money... As I look back, it is this one measure that was responsible for many from my generation to live a less stressful life today.

As the world becomes borderless and the chase for talent becomes relentless, you have to learn to become a citizen of the world, not just of Singapore ...

Balji is not an emotional person, but the letter betrays an emotionally literate man who can dig deep to show how he feels, in his own way. It was a long letter, written from the depth of a grandfather's heart, arising from the kind of "rough patch" that allowed the grandson to truly see his grandfather for who he really was. While he said he could not express his love for his grandson the way his wife could, the letter nevertheless went beyond mere expression of love. Nakedly honest,

Grandchildren: Arrian and Roman.

earnest and straight, the characteristic way he would talk to anyone he cares deeply for. Although the man could not come right out to say "I love you, grandson", it was nevertheless, his manly tough love, wrapped thoughtfully with advice for what his grandson would need in life. From his future spouse ("it is very important that you choose your life partner based on values") to complexities in relationships ("learn to adapt and compromise"), children ("... children bring tremendous joy to your life; your life will become more balanced and meaningful.") and, of course, world affairs ("You cannot just think local; global is the name of the game.").

Balji ended off the letter on the subject of family:

> In the end, family is everything. Your family members
> are the only ones who will love you without bias and
> support you at all cost. If I am asked to pin down the
> values you need in a brave new world, I would pick
> these two: wings and roots. They sound contradictory,
> but they are not. Wings for you to fly, roots for you to
> know that if you have any problems, you can always go
> back to your roots – your home – to find solace.

The newsroom has taken up more than four decades of his life. It has moulded and, in many ways, defined him. Today, long after leaving it behind, people still remember Balji as the veteran newsman. Only those close by, his family and a handful of old friends, know that the newsman is well into his second act – a keen observer and commentator of news and current affairs, and a scholar of grand-fatherhood.

"The most liberating aspect of not working for a big corporation and working for myself is that I am independent," the words come out slowly, each possessed of a joy that is almost private to him. "When I was with SPH, when I was with MediaCorp, there were always lines I knew I could not cross: the first was the company's sensitivities, then the government's sensitivities. Today, when I write as a contributor to *Yahoo* or *The New Singapore*, I represent myself mostly. I am responsible for the views expressed, the arguments I put forth and the conclusions made. What I say I must be able to defend."

He has guarded his independence jealously his entire life. Today, this independence sets him apart from other commentators. He has developed a voice the public looks out for: a balanced, considered and original voice that is rare in Singapore.

NOTES

1   Woon Tai Ho, *Soul of Ink: Lim Tze Peng at 100* (World Scientific, 2021).

2   Woon Tai Ho, PN Balji, Keith Nakamura & Eugene Quah, *We Have a Problem: Crisis and Reputation Management in the Digital Age* (Candid Creation Publishing, 2016).

3   Felix Cheong (ed), *Letter to My Son: Words of wisdom, advice and lessons on life from parents* (Marshall Cavendish Editions, 2020).

Chapter 5

A Political Limbo

The ruling party at a crossroad

Warning sign

It is the first Monday of March, and Balji wants to take me to a new coffee shop. Good, a change of scene. I meet him outside his house at 8.15am. "We'll take a walk, just a little further from the usual place," he assures me. Four hundred metres later, the new coffee shop appears. It occupies the entire ground floor of a relatively new office building. M38 @ Jalan Pemimpin is a light business and industrial development, nine floors with a charming façade. It stands out simply by being new, amidst old and worn-out neighbours. At 8.30am, the place feels lonely. Only one Malay and three Chinese stalls are open; the two of us join a handful of early birds for breakfast.

A white rooster by the side of the road surprises me; it looks on, unsure if it wants to get closer. Jalan Pemimpin may be a light industrial enclave but it is also close to Clover Way, a residential area where wild fowls like this white rooster are allowed to roam. "I like this place," I say, as the morning sun streams in, lifting me. The rooster suddenly becomes interested in the crumbs on the next table and decides to switch allegiance.

At most coffee shops, the stall that sells drinks is the busiest. But at this hour, being among the very few customers there, our *kopi c* and *teh c kosong* are whipped up in seconds.

March is the month when the weather starts to get warm, and the morning sun is giving us ample warning. Without any clouds in the sky, this Monday promises to be the beginning of our hot and humid season.

"I got my first jab," says Balji, looking happy, referring to the Covid-19 vaccination roll-out in Singapore, first to seniors, then to the rest of the population who are 16 years old and above. "The nurse told me, no alcohol after vaccination, for two whole days!" I am quietly excited; vaccination brings with it a kind of freedom. I should be getting my notice to be vaccinated soon.

The planned and orderly lives of Singaporeans contrast dramatically with the chaos and despair Covid-19 has brought to neighbouring countries. In Myanmar, everyone is consumed by the bigger drama – the military coup. Protests there persist for the sixth week and have gone horribly wrong. The escalating situation continues to dominate the news, especially the death of Kyal Sin, a 19-year-old girl given the nickname "Angel".

The scene was clearly described in an NPR Opinion article by Scott Simon:[1]

> The photo of Kyal Sin at that demonstration has been seen around the world by now. A young girl on the ground, reaching out, crouching behind protest banners, and wearing a T-shirt that says, "Everything will be OK."
>
> But police fired tear gas. Shooting started from security forces. Kyal Sin shouted, "Are we united?" and the protesters around her shouted back, in a chant, "United! United!"

Her friend Myat Thu told Reuters that Kyal Sin kicked
open a water pipe so protesters could wash tear gas
from their eyes. …

The police opened fire and she was shot in the head. Simon
then refers to the impact of this brutal slaying:[2]

The last images of Kyal Sin, the teenage girl known as
Angel, may stir memories from other images in history,
of innocent and hopeful young people, crushed by
brutal events.

Neda Agha-Soltan, the young woman shot on the edge
of election protests in Tehran in 2009. Admira Ismic
and Bosko Brkic, the young couple shot in 1993 as they
tried to dash across a bridge in Sarajevo to a place where
their love between a Muslim and Serb would be safe. …

In the case of Kyal Sin, her life was so abruptly cut
short, which angered many Myanmar protesters,
fuelling their resolve to fight on in her name.

"Both sides are digging in," says Balji, who follows the
development of the region keenly, and Myanmar is now the
country everyone focuses on. "Every day, new episodes erupt,
anchoring their resolve; the military will be more brutal and
the protesters more defiant. Outside mediation, especially
from ASEAN, is crucial. Singapore's responses, first from
the Foreign Ministry and most recently from PM Lee, have
been strong. Singapore has been unusually vocal." I can tell
he is pleasantly surprised by how Singapore has led in the call
for the Myanmar military to halt its aggression on its own
civilians.

The upsurge of youthful anger in the face of military intervention in Myanmar prompts an uneasy question: will this ever happen in Singapore? Violence in Singapore seems far-fetched, at least for now and the immediate future. But the military in every country needs to be appeased, kept happy, and Singapore is no different. In fact, there is a "civilian" component of the military in Singapore politics that many know but few want to highlight. "The role of the military in Singapore is unlike anywhere else in the world," Balji takes a sip of his *kopi c.* "Top military personalities retire relatively young and get senior political and administrative positions. Many Cabinet ministers were from the military. The Prime Minister was a Brigadier-General for a long time. Not very long ago, all PAP candidates were either from the admin service or the military."

The Myanmar situation puts Balji in a reflective mood. What about young people in Singapore? "What kind of future do young people have in Singapore?" he wonders out loud. "The questions they ask, their references, their whole mindset are different from our political leaders. Our leaders are not in sync with them. The younger generation has an international outlook because of the Internet and social media. Unlike their parents, they do not just accept what the leaders tell them. Politics in Singapore, while it may appear to have embraced universal liberal values, is still locked in a philosophy that the PAP started out with, in the 1960s and 1970s, one that is dangerously outdated."

From the founding political elite to the current 4th Generation or 4G leaders, Singapore leaders have never made any attempt to hide the fact that they do not see liberal democracy to have high value for Singapore. They have established a domestic political paradigm based on foundations that do not match with the liberal democracy of the West.

Ian P. Austin, in his 2009 article, referred to Singapore as being "commonly defined as an 'administrative state'"

> … consisting of politicians and a selected elite bureaucracy-intelligentsia, who themselves often enter politics through the PAP, this elite apparatchik defines what is in the best interest of the Singapore citizen. The focus is nearly completely materialistic, with a driving interest on delivering to that citizenship dramatically improved housing, employment opportunity, infrastructure, education and national strategic security. The role of the elite bureaucracy, fully under the control of the PAP hierarchy and often destined to become members of it, is particularly noticeable as they take on the role of policy makers, as opposed to the policy-enacting role subscribed to them within the liberal model.[3]

"The PAP has been in power for so long, it permeates through every aspects of our lives," Balji says, his view best captured by Austin in his article:[4]

> Singaporeans are constantly reminded that, in a hostile world, only the PAP leadership has the experience and wherewithal to guide the Singapore ship safely to shore. …

> The creative minds defined as crucial to the new economy of Singapore are not only completely absent from the political centre, but they are often completely ignored by it, or, indeed, besieged by it. …

... the political predominance of PAP group-think, its obsessive commitment to scientific technocracy to the exclusion of almost all other skill sets from the higher reaches of office, poses a risk management threat to the long-term future of the Singaporean economy.

Austin goes on to point out:[5]

There has been much talk of political renewal within the PAP over the previous decade, without much change in the collective thinking and backgrounds of the political participants incorporated into the cabinet or other higher echelon positions within the PAP or government.

"They maintain that they are pragmatic and have made provisions within the system to incorporate alternative ideas by including former critics into significant government boards and statutory authorities," Balji leans back, slowly pursing his lips. "And there is, of course, the other strategy, one that has proven to be controversial, one that remains like an albatross around their necks: ministerial salaries. The idea is to pay ministers and top public servants salaries that match those of their MNC counterparts. This is to allow them to recruit and retain the best candidates to steer Singapore forward. But it will not change anything if these candidates go through the same selection process, contributing to the same group-think."

Every four years, during the general elections, the considerable strengths but perhaps also the increasing weaknesses of the PAP are on show. The PAP were running against ten parties and one independent candidate in the

2020 General Election. The results and implications are set out in an article by Nigel Li:[6]

> During the 2011 general election, the PAP saw their vote share dip to 60.1 per cent, their lowest ever performance. The 61.24 per cent result brings the PAP uncomfortably close to their 2011 days. This is a setback from the gains made in the 2015 general election, where the PAP gained 69.9 per cent of the votes.

Observers such as Li have attributed the upsurge in support in 2015 to the following:[7]

> … the "feel good factor" due to celebrations of Singapore's 50th year of independence (SG50) and the passing of Singapore's first Prime Minister Lee Kuan Yew. There was no SG50 or Lee Kuan Yew factor to bolster the PAP during the 2020 general election.

"Elections are often seen as referendum of a ruling party, and in Singapore's case, the performance of the PAP," says Balji, agreeing with Li's view that "the results for Deputy Prime Minister and Finance Minister Heng Swee Keat, set to be Singapore's next prime minister, are rather telling." Staring straight ahead, he continues, "Against the Workers' Party team at East Coast GRC, he only managed 53.41 per cent of the votes. If you compare this to PM Lee Hsien Loong's win of 71.91 per cent in the Ang Mo Kio GRC, the writing is definitely on the wall."

Senior Minister Tharman Shanmugaratnam has been one of the most popular politicians in Singapore, with some hoping that he will be the next prime minister. However, Heng Swee Keat had gone public saying a segment of Singaporeans would not be ready for a prime minister who was not Chinese.[8] "We are multiracial, a statement like that would definitely draw attention not just around the world and in the region, but from the other racial groups in Singapore," Balji points out. "Tharman won 74.62 per cent of the votes in Jurong GRC, he performed better than the current PM and the other PAP candidates. Between the PM designate and Tharman was a 21.1 percentage gap, perhaps Heng Swee Keat should not have said what he said."

The ten elected Opposition seats, while a small number compared to the PAP's 83, was nonetheless "big" in the Singapore context, with WP under a new leader making an impact.

Balji agrees with Li's assessment:[9]

[T]he gains made in the 2020 general election are a significant victory for the opposition, and a warning sign to the PAP. The ruling government will not only have to deal with the Covid-19 pandemic but will also have to win back the hearts and minds of the many voters that left them.

He concludes, "People have said that politics in Singapore is boring, sterile and dull. Well, the 2020 polls proved otherwise. If anything, Singaporeans have proven to such cynics that democracy in Singapore is alive and well, and politics here is anything but sterile."

From miracle to complacency

A former BBC World Service journalist, Nicholas Walton lived in Singapore for over three years. During his time here, he walked across the island in one day and produced a book entitled, *Singapore, Singapura: From Miracle to Complacency*.[10] His one-day walk, 53km from one end of the island to the other in 2017, worked as a literary device because Singaporeans, according to him, did not really "do walking". Through the book, Walton gave readers a glimpse of the Singaporean as portrayed in the film *Crazy Rich Asians* – materialistic and carefree. As the blisters developed and his feet started to bleed, Walton asked the questions: what are the human and environmental costs of Singapore's success, and are they sustainable?[11]

Writing fluently and engagingly, it was a somewhat coloured but unflinching portrayal of Singapore and its people seen through an expatriate lens (all of three years, Walton's praises were always grudging and qualified, and his criticisms fell squarely into the predictable Western liberal cocoon). At parts light with a sense of humour, it was more than a travelogue. As reviewer James Brabazon called it, "a grand adventure told in the tradition of Conrad with the eye of Theroux and the wit of Bryson." Walton noted that modern Singapore was a "miracle", given its lack of natural resources and small size but wondered whether the nation's achievements had "bred a dangerous sense of complacency among Singapore's people".

From the title of the book, Walton suggested that Singapore's leaders had lost the ability to adapt and innovate as they had done so successfully in the past to maintain the island's prosperity and security. Empires and economic cycles come and go, and there is obviously a risk that Singapore will one day decline. Pointing out that there was talk of a "Singapore model" in the globalised world today, Walton said there were "challenges ahead, from public complacency and the constraints of authoritarian democracy to changing geographic realities and the difficulties of balancing migration in such a tiny state."

Miracle, of course. Singapore leaders have been quick to use the term many times, to describe an unbelievable state of being.

Walton continued:[12]

Half a century ago, it was thrown out of the Malay Federation and unwillingly became an independent nation. It was tiny, poor, almost devoid of resources, and in a hostile neighbourhood. Now, this unlikely country is at the top of almost every global national index, from high wealth and low crime to superb education and much-envied stability. But have these achievements bred a dangerous sense of complacency?

"With success, especially on this scale, there will be complacency," it is clear Balji does not fully subscribe to Walton's broad-stroke thesis. "The problem is more serious than complacency. The party has not changed since the 1960s and the 1970s, it is not in sync with a new generation who are not the same as their parents. They rely on the same means of recruiting new members into their party, their group-think is their Achilles' heel."

An example of how out of sync the government is with the general public: on Sunday, 4 April 2021, a blogger announced that he had raised $133,000 in only 11 days of crowdfunding on social media to cover damages he had been ordered to pay Prime Minister Lee Hsien Loong in a defamation case filed by the city-state's leader. Lee had sued Leong Sze Hian, a financial advisor, after he shared on Facebook an online news article that linked the premier to a financial scandal at Malaysia's state fund 1MDB. Lee's lawyers have said such links were "false and baseless". Leong deleted the November 2018 Facebook post within three days of sharing it, complying with a government request. On 24 March 2021, the Singapore High Court ordered him to pay Lee $133,000 in damages.

Leong made the announcement of the success of his crowdfunding effort on Facebook late on Sunday, when he posted, "It is finished. All paid for … Miracle on Easter Sunday," and noted that 2,065 people had contributed to the crowdfunding effort, with the highest donation at $5,000 and the smallest at $2.91.

As the head of a government that has pledged zero tolerance for corruption, Lee is no stranger to seeking protection of his reputation via legal channels. Senior figures in the ruling PAP, including his late father, Lee Kuan Yew, have previously sued foreign media, political opponents and online commentators for defamation.

"It's a p-y-r-r-h-i-c victory," says Balji, spelling the word out. A "pyrrhic" victory is a victory that inflicts such a devastating toll on the victor that it is tantamount to defeat. In war, it could mean heavy casualties, or "victory" attained after so many years that one questions if it was worth the suffering and losses incurred.

This, Balji thinks, is just one of many signs that the PAP continues to behave in ways that show they are no longer in touch with the people of Singapore. "We live in a very fast-paced environment, developments in the media are updated in real-time on social media, the voice of the everyday man, who once did not have the chance to be heard. Today they are not only heard, they can make a difference to outcomes of public debates and policies. It is a new reality that cannot be ignored. If the PAP thinks it is above this, then it is headed for disappointment, even failure, at each and every turn. In my opinion, the Leong Sze Hian crowdfunding success shows that the public can nullify what the PAP is doing and has been doing for decades."

With the PAP, it has always been top-down, not bottom-up. Balji continues, "There is a fundamental need for Singapore society to rebuild its capacity to take risks and learn from its failures, though this goes against ingrained conservatism and conformism." What is most needed at this stage is "to rebuild society's capacity for rigorous self-inspection, empowering individuals and non-public sector actors to experiment. Such actors can highlight trends the public sector may overlook or underestimate. Furthermore, they should have the freedom to question policies more deeply, rather than simply relying on government information and data. The world today is much more complex than the world 50 years ago when Singapore was founded. At that time, the population was less educated and depended on the handful of well-qualified leaders to build a nation. Today, not all the best talents are in government, they are everywhere in society. The government no longer has the sole wisdom in solving future problems.

"The people need to play a bigger role in nation building and the government needs to trust the people more and be prepared to share the stage with the non-public sector actors." Even as he makes these suggestions, he knows it will be futile unless there is a rebel, perhaps a few, within the ruling PAP party to change the approach to the group-think.

Heng Swee Keat

One topic that has consumed Balji since the 2020 General Election is the political succession of Singapore, from the 3rd Generation or 3G to 4th Generation or 4G leaders. When Heng Swee Keat announced that he was taking himself out of running as the Prime Minister of Singapore, Balji saw it as the first succession crisis in Singapore's political history.

Thursday evening, 8 April 2021. Prime Minister Lee Hsien Loong opens a press conference acknowledging that Heng Swee Keat, Deputy Prime Minister and the person designated by the ruling PAP to one day succeed Lee, is no longer in the running for the position. Although the Singapore public may not entirely expect Heng to actually succeed Lee, the announcement nevertheless comes as a jolt. If nothing else, it is tough to watch a man raised so high only to be allowed to fall so low.

The Prime Minister speaks for over a minute, then invites Heng to speak. The camera pans to Heng, who is seen fumbling around with the microphone, unsure of how to turn it on. "You press [the button]," the Prime Minister orders like an impatient teacher. This, of course, brings back memories of a November 2019 parliamentary session, when Lee was seen, face knotted with annoyance, coaching Heng on how to joust with the Opposition's Sylvia Lim, like a general issuing orders to his colonel in full view of the enemy. Nicholas Yong of *Yahoo News* described this vividly:[13]

> Having proposed a motion that called on Workers' Party (WP) Members of Parliament (MP) Low Thia Khiang and Sylvia Lim to recuse themselves from financial matters relating to Aljunied-Hougang Town Council (AHTC), he was supposed to carry the ball. …

Instead, just minutes into the debate on the motion, Heng had to call for a time-out. He hummed and hawed, flipping through his folder like a student stumbling through his class presentation.

"The video of PM Lee looking exasperated and instructing Heng on what to say in the session has been circulating online," Balji shakes his head slowly. "It was painful to watch the next Prime Minister so lost and unprepared. Looking back, it was Lee Hsien Loong's fleeting reaction that should have made Singaporeans sit back and ask: can Heng become our leader? The video showed the PM using his laptop to coach his deputy, probably on what to say. Before Lee could finish, Heng stood up to respond to Lim. And Lee threw his head back in exasperation."

Today, nearly two years later, as Singaporeans talk about Heng's decision to step aside, that video is featuring as the moment that could have sealed Heng's fate. But the party cadres backed Heng a year ago and gave him the most number of votes to be the 4G leader. This endorsement gave him the position of the first assistant secretary general of the PAP.

"That decision has an intriguing back story," says Balji, who has written about Heng's accession to PM-in-waiting for many news platforms. "The voting results were leaked to *Lian He Zaobao* one day before the party leadership had made it official. The talk was that many cadres had feared that a re-vote might be ordered and Chan Chun Sing would pip Heng to the post and become the first assistant secretary general. I had written a commentary in *Yahoo* then, saying Heng must return the favour and show those cadres who went against tradition to leak the story that he will be a different leader and introduce changes that a modern society like Singapore needs."

Alas, that was not to be as Heng fumbled in the 2020 General Election and his vote share of 53 per cent was the lowest for a minister. His reasons for stepping aside – like his age at 60 which gave him a shorter runway to deal with the debilitating effects of the Covid-19 pandemic – can be easily dismissed. Many analysts have done that already.

"For the good of Singapore, the discussion should move further to whether the country's much cherished and well-choreographed political succession has gone haywire," Balji's dry voice breaks, sounding almost sad that it has come to this. "The process was the envy of the world with the element of unpredictability totally absent. Long before first Prime Minister Lee Kuan Yew stepped aside, we knew Goh Chok Tong would take over. And when Goh became PM, we knew Lee Hsien Loong was the anointed successor." He pauses. "See how different the situation is today. After being in power for 17 years, we still don't know who will take over from Lee Hsien Loong." Balji pushes his chair out, folds his arms and lets his head fall back.

Is there a way out of this deadlock? Balji goes back to what he has said before. The criteria of selection must change. The leadership must stay relevant to a new Singapore, and Singapore needs a rebel or rebels within its highest ranks. The system needs a jolt, someone who is not part of the group-think.

"It is very clear that the ruling party's pick of the political crop is getting weaker at each election cycle. Yet, nobody wants to take the bull by its horns and ask for a review of the selection criteria. Start looking for people who have not only achieved scholastic feats but also those with a warm touch and an ability to communicate with the common man earnestly. And those who have an empathetic ear to listen to people's problems.

"More importantly, within its rank and file, there must be those who are not scared to speak up against established thinking on policies. Singapore needs a few rebels, constructive rebels, let me add, to get our leaders to think out of the box. Under Lee Hsien Loong's leadership, the quality of political talent has been going down. The missteps and embarrassments are too many. Singapore's top terrorist, Mas Selmat, escaped. The ruling party suffered a huge blow when it recorded a historic low of 60.1 per cent of the share of popular vote in 2011. The decision to open the floodgates to foreigners despite complaints from Singaporeans had many asking if the country has competent leaders. Under the current leadership, the ruling party lost its first GRC in 2011 and then another last year. And on the day Heng announced his surprise decision to step aside came the news that more than $300 million in job subsidies were paid by mistake to companies hit by Covid-19.

"Now that the Prime Minister is likely to stay on in his job for a while longer, here is a historic opportunity to reboot his political vision. He must not forget that Singapore society is changing. The enormous public support blogger Leong Sze Hian received in paying off the damages he suffered in his libel suit by the Prime Minister is just one sign of a new society emerging. And, to add, those who gave money to his cause did so without any sense of fear."

On 12 July 2021, one year after the 2020 General Election, Balji writes a commentary for *Yahoo News*:[14]

Two images pop up every time I think about GE2020 – for very different reasons. One shows Leader of the Opposition Pritam Singh taking to the camera on the last day of election campaigning and the other is that of Finance Minister and the man who was designated to be the next Prime Minister, Heng Swee Keat, fumbling his speech on Nomination Day.

They show how an opposition party has managed its leadership renewal smoothly while the ruling party has stumbled, fallen down and stumbled again as the race for prime minister-ship continues to be muddled. One year after GE2020 and Singapore has still not got the one thing that it always gets right; political succession is still stuck in the mud.

But if there is one name that stands out among the 4G leaders, it is the new Finance Minister, Lawrence Wong. And in his own cryptic way, is Balji hinting that Wong could be suitable as the next Prime Minister?

"The last two prime ministers had been Finance Ministers," Balji says whimsically. "Finance Minister Lawrence Wong has hardly put a wrong foot forward as he has become the public face in the battle against Covid-19. He exudes confidence and communicates clearly and with a permanent smile on his face. His speech on race at a recent forum again put on display a politician who is prepared to move slightly away from the establishment's line of thinking. The 4G leadership knows that hardliners in Cabinet are waiting to pounce on them if they stray too far away from PAP's ideology. It is this game they must win if Singapore is to enter a new era of governance and politics."

Here's looking at you, Lawrence Wong.

NOTES

1   Scott Simon, "Opinion: Death Of A Teenage Protester in Myanmar", NPR Opinion, 6 March 2021 <https://www.npr.org/2021/03/06/974248374/opinion-death-of-a-teenage-protester-in-myanmar>.

2   See note 1.

3   Ian P. Austin, "Singapore in transition: economic change and political consequences", *Journal of Asian Public Policy* (2009) 2:3, 266–278; published online 18 November 2009 <https://www.tandfonline.com/doi/full/10.1080/17516230903204745#>.

4   See note 3.

5   See note 3.

6   Nigel Li, "A 'New Mandate' for Singapore's Government?" *The Diplomat*, 13 July 2020 <https://thediplomat.com/2020/07/a-new-mandate-for-singapores-government/>.

7   See note 6.

8   Wong Pei Ting, "Older generation of S'poreans not ready for non-Chinese PM: Heng Swee Keat", Today, 29 March 2019 <https://www.todayonline.com/singapore/older-generation-singaporeans-not-ready-non-chinese-pm-heng-swee-keat>.

9   See note 6.

10 Nicholas Walton, *Singapore, Singapura: From Miracle to Complacency* (Hurst & Co, 2018).

11 Victor Mallet, "Singapore, Singapura: From Miracle to Complacency by Nicholas Walton", *Financial Times*, 10 June 2019 <https://www.ft.com/content/fbbb28d2-885c-11e9-97ea-05ac2431f453>.

12 See note 10; quote from book cover blurb.

13 Nicholas Yong, "Comment: Heng Swee Keat needs to raise his game against Workers' Party", *Yahoo News*, 6 November 2019 <https://sg.news.yahoo.com/comment-heng-swee-keat-needs-to-raise-his-game-against-workers-party-120616036.html>.

14 PN Balji, "Comment: Singapore politics one year after GE2020", *Yahoo News*, 12 July 2021 <https://sg.news.yahoo.com/singapore-politics-one-year-ge-2020-121731086.html>.

Chapter 6

The Modern Family

It is the emotional ties that hold hearts together

Roman's version of family includes his grandparents.

Pool in the sky

In the end, family is everything. Your family members are the only ones who will love you without bias and support you at all cost. If I am asked to pin down the values you need in a brave new world, I would pick these two: wings and roots. They sound contradictory, but they are not. Wings for you to fly, roots for you to know that if you have any problems, you can always go back to your roots – your home – to find solace.

> – Extract from PN Balji's letter to his grandson,
>   from *Letter to My Son*

This is the anchoring thought in Balji's letter to his grandson, Arrian (see Chapter 4). It captures two seemingly divergent perspectives, of deliverance and return. But it also captures the very essence of the modern family, which is no longer about geography, where home is a place, town or country. More and more, a family is about emotional ties that hold hearts together. And with the help of technology, it is easier to be in touch with your roots, no matter how far and high you fly.

When it comes to marriage and family, I must confess, Balji can be an enigma. Is he a conservative or liberal? He does not regret that his was an arranged marriage, yet when it comes to his daughters and their life partners, you can tag him as a Western liberal. Have as many boyfriends as possible before you settle down, was his advice to his daughters. Perhaps beneath the modern exterior hides a traditionalist, but a very practical one. Just like his words to Arrian – fly, but know we will always be here if you fall.

Exploring what it means to be in Balji's family brings me to a place I have always wanted to visit. I am excited. I like unusual architectural designs and this morning, I am visiting one by world famous architect Moshe Safdie, who happens to be responsible for Marina Bay Sands and a holocaust museum in Israel. When it was launched in 2012, Sky Habitat was considered the most expensive suburban condominium, with transacted prices of around $1,580 per square foot. It is the tallest skyscraper in the Bishan area, with a rooftop Sky Pool on the 38th floor.

9.30am. I get off at Bishan station on the North-South line and instead of turning left for Clover Way, I turn right, across the Junction 8 mall. From a distance, Sky Habitat looks bottom heavy, pregnant around the base and becoming progressively slimmer as it rises upwards. Two other architectural wonders in Singapore quickly come to mind: Reflections at Keppel Bay and The Interlace. I had photographed them for my Instagram account. The Interlace in particular stretches my imagination with random overlapping blocks. What is Sky Habitat like, up close?

Security is tight. I have to give my particulars and reason for visiting. The guard, wearing a serious look, walks me to a side gate. "Block 7 is straight ahead," he declares with authority. The estate looks brand new even though it was launched almost a decade ago. The well-publicised three-dimensional matrix of homes, gardens, terraces and sky bridges are coming to life right before me.

Deepa Balji, Balji and Uma's eldest daughter, is in her 40s. She is married to Sri Jegarajah, the broadcast anchor of CNBC. They have two children, Arrian and Roman. As usual, I am early; the apartment on the ninth floor is large, with many sources of light streaming in and through the unit.

"We bought a four-room apartment because we need to think ahead, elder-care," says Deepa. "We want our home to be available to both Sri's parents and mine, especially when they are getting on in their years." I am touched and impressed – a daughter makes plans for her own family with her parents in mind. Extended family planning, tradition is alive and well.

Even on the ninth floor, the apartment has an unblocked view. Above the dining table is a sculpture that doubles as a lamp, with three light shades sitting on a trunk. The light at night must be unusual, I tell myself. "Everyone comments on the lamp," Deepa smiles as she offers me cold water. "We can go up to the pool for a chat." Ah, the famous Sky Pool.

Sri, in his three-piece suit, walks in, surprising Deepa. "Oh good, you're back." The anchor of CNBC wakes up at three in the morning to be in the office in time for the early morning breakfast show. Visibly exhausted, he excuses himself while Deepa and I make our way to the Sky Pool.

"It hasn't been easy," Deepa begins, looking at the long stretch of very blue water, which forms part of the bridging sky garden that connects the estate's two blocks. Both of us are hiding in the shade afforded by palm trees that line the 50-metre infinity pool. It is 11am, the early morning swimmers have gone; we are the only ones up on the rooftop. "The Balji name has a kind of instant recognition, you are automatically put in a place where people think or feel they know you just because of your surname. You are conferred this 'celebrity' status, if you like, without having to prove yourself or show what you can do or potentially do." The burden of being the child of a well-known name: there is jealousy, envy, even resentment. "I remember applying for a job at MediaCorp and Chandra Mohan, the director of Current Affairs, did not want to be on the interview panel because he knew my father." Deepa was eventually an on-air talent and correspondent for Channel NewsAsia, the news channel of MediaCorp. She is now with an MNC, S4 Capital. "I like to think I am now my own person. Balji is just my last name."

Beyond the burden of name, she admits that being the daughter of Balji and Uma is a privilege she cherishes. In her mind, her father is not just "Dad", but a cool man who told her to have as many as 32 boyfriends before she settled down, someone she could talk to about everything including her periods and also someone who has achieved success in a field she too has chosen for herself – journalism.

The wind is strong on the rooftop, Deepa's fingers tame her hair and she turns her face away from the gushing wind. "The biggest hurdle for fathers is when their daughters start menstruating. Most feel that they need to stay away as it's a 'female' thing, leaving it to mothers to handle. My father saw it as an opportunity to get and stay close, being empathetic to the cramps and the hormonal ride. So much so that he became a pro at it in the process. And when my younger sister started having her period, he could guess due to the breakout of pimples. But more important, he made us feel it wasn't something 'dirty' that we should be ashamed of. He told us not to ban ourselves from going to the temple just because we had our periods."

And growing up, it was clear to her that her parents took an active interest in every aspect of her life. "I had an eclectic group of friends while growing up. Some were black, others loved whisky, and most were gay. My parents took a special interest in my friends, some of whom they knew from my childhood. In fact, my mother became quite close to my gay friends. They remained curious, asking a lot of questions as they navigated this colourful terrain in my life. They were supportive of my choices and always wanted to know my friends better."

There are one or two personal episodes that she still holds close to her heart. "I am probably one of the very few girls who grew up knowing that my father took pains to spend time with me," Deepa looks at me, a grin appearing on her face. "I remember looking at his Filofax and there it was, 'spend time with Deepa' written on several parts of his day and week. This is despite carrying the cross of running newspapers and pressured newsroom operations in Singapore. In fact, my father carved out time to fly to England, where I was a student. The best memory I have is watching Nabokov's *Lolita* with him in one of London's independent theatres."

With Balji and Uma as her parents, how have they affected her own parenting?

"If there is one difference between my parents' generation and mine, and how the parenting differs, it is how open and free we are with our children. There was a time when Arrian was younger and he made homophobic comments. For Sri and I, it was a no-no. That was when we decided that he should watch 'Modern Family'. And over time, his comments changed."

What are her aspirations for her children?

"We want the children to be race agnostic; our home environment is free, open and we try to bring them up without boundaries. For this reason, we had to bring Arrian out of a government school and into an international school. It is a growth mindset; we don't want them to have any restrictions. From the questions he asks, we know the change of school was the right move."

It is clear that, like her mother, Deepa excels in the things she chooses to do. And like her mother, she is also emotionally open, every bit a woman and also a corporate go-getter. Despite, or because of the Balji name, she is a successful career woman embodying both the yin and yang forces of her father and mother. Modern in almost every sense of the word, yet there is also tradition running in her blood. All grown up and a mother in her own right, yet it is the daughter's voice that I hear when she speaks of her parents. Even though her family is now a modern family, I sense that her approach to family has roots in tradition. She may have adjusted her wings and flown, but she is keenly aware of where she is from. Up high on the rooftop by the Sky Pool, if I look down hard enough, I can see Clover Way. The apple, as they say, doesn't fall far from the tree.

Then and now

As a child, I remember watching one of the earliest sitcoms on TV, "Father Knows Best". Robert Young starred as Jim Anderson, an agent for the General Insurance Company, who lived with his wife, Margaret, and their three children at 607 South Maple Lane in Springfield, a wholesome Midwestern suburban community. The stories revolved around the various exploits of the Anderson family, whose problems were neatly resolved in each 30-minute episode by listening to Father (and, by extension, Mother) and doing the right thing.

Over a 20-year period from the 1970s, reruns of "Father Knows Best" have frequently been seen on television, offering a dose of nostalgia to the baby boomers who came of age watching this almost perfect suburban family. Like many sitcoms of that period, it came to acquire the camp appeal of the quaintly outmoded, particularly in its treatment of gender issues. Women knew their place in the Anderson family (and in 1950s America), and in the rare instances when they momentarily lost sight of their place, some revelatory incident would gently nudge them back into submission, because "Father knows best". Predictably, it was the archetypal representation of the 1950s ideal of family life, and came to be regarded as an important influence on American family values.

Fast forward four decades …

A sitcom arrived in 2009, surprising everyone with its success, including its creators: it lasted 11 years, ending only in 2020. In a bizarre yet logical way, it is the closest to an accurate reflection of what constitutes the modern family today. Simply titled "Modern Family" (of course), it featured Jay, an old rich man remarried to a younger Colombian woman named Gloria (who had her own son), with two adult children of his own, Claire and Mitchell. Claire and her husband, Phil, had three children, while Mitchell and his gay partner, Cameron, had adopted a Vietnamese baby. The three families were "modern" in every sense of the word: each family unit was small, multiracial and multicultural, and every family member was a "personality".

Modern families, as opposed to the traditional ones, are made up of members who are equal, regardless of age, gender or sexual orientation. In the sitcom, everyone had an opinion, including the six-year-old. Diversity was not just tolerated, it was prized. Children and teenagers, and how they are inducted into adulthood, are often at the centre of modern families. In a typical modern family, one would not necessarily take care of only his or her own children, you could be a grandparent or step-parent. When I ask Balji for his definition of the modern family, he brings it back to the Singapore context.

"I am sure there are many views, not just one definition. The family I started way back in the 1970s was pretty traditional," he sits back. "For most Singaporeans, given the high cost of living today, a modern family is one where both the husband and wife work."

How do children and their upbringing come into this definition? Who takes care of them when both parents work?

"I think that's the part parents haven't figured out the

answer to, most parents that is." Balji makes a point to talk to as many people as possible; it is not unusual for him to strike up conversations with strangers on a bus, asking them about their children and families. "If a couple can afford it, one of them should stay at home and see the children through their formative years. My daughter, Deepa, is lucky: Sri, being an anchor on TV, is back home at 9am, when she leaves for work. That way, one of them is always home. But when they are both busy, the one person or persons available to stand in are the grandparents, Uma and I."

Marriage and family are two topics close to his heart. "I hope the definition of modern family does not include 'no family'." The institution of marriage is something he feels deeply about. "You know me," he smiles. "I will always encourage marriage, preferably early marriage and having children early. I see what marriage and children have done for my eldest daughter, Deepa. She deals with people differently now that she is a wife, and especially after she became a mother. She is calmer and altogether a more wholesome person, a better person."

I am reminded of what Sofia Vergara, the actress who became a breakout star playing the feisty Gloria in "Modern Family", said about family: "Despite everything that's going on in life, I really hope the show reminds people how important family is."

Not just important, but central to Balji's world: family is at the heart of both the health of individuals and the health of societies. Crucially, the health of a family unit is central to the education of children and how children become well-adjusted adults. Well-functioning families are therefore central to stable communities, which are the building blocks of society and of democracy, too. "In all countries, in all societies, the family unit is central to its ultimate stability. A country with good families is a strong country. Which is why when we talk about the modern family, I worry. Every so often, the most important part of family is sacrificed in the name of modernity and progress."

Census 2020 (conducted every ten years and surveyed 150,000 households in 2020) reflected profound changes in attitudes towards marriage and parenthood, with fewer Singaporeans getting married and having children compared to ten years ago, and with younger Singaporeans more likely to stay single. The census showed singlehood has become more prevalent across multiple age groups over the last decade, particularly among younger Singaporeans aged 25 to 34. The country is also getting older and is experiencing its slowest decade of population growth since independence. Between 2010 and 2020, the population increased by 1.1 per cent a year, a slowdown from the 2.5 per cent per year between 2000 and 2010.

What aspects of the traditional family should still be kept, if it is possible at all? Balji laughs. "I see many friends and children of friends, young girls choosing to marry late and having children even later. It is not something I can change because it is the trend. Women want their professional aspirations fulfilled first, then their personal and parental aspirations later. It should be reversed. But the young people listening to me will not agree, most of them anyway. It was just in the newspapers; the birthrate is at a record ten-year low. Another perennial problem that is chronically part of modern Singapore."

In a traditional family, marriage was contracted by the

parents. The marriage contract was based on the principal of male dominance and female obedience. In a modern family, people are less subject to parental control concerning whom and when they should marry. Marriage is now settled by the partners themselves. It is a personal choice, usually preceded by courtship and then falling in love.

"In arranged marriages, compatible partnership was sought. So, people didn't marry necessarily for love, but found love after marriage," Balji says with an even voice. He knows what young people think about arranged marriages but is in no mood to apologise for it. "In other words, the wife and husband tried to find ways to love each other, find reasons to stay together. The passage of time helped. It could be moving into their new home, when the children arrived. The proverbial building of a life together, piece by piece. There was no pressure of time, no ticking of the biological body clock. For me and Uma, we had the luxury of time on our side, discovering and building our home together, enjoying our children as they grew up while we were relatively young, and then being a part of our children's family. We had time because we had an early start. And the fact that Uma didn't work helped."

In the modern family, the woman is not the devotee of the man but an equal partner in life with equal rights. The husband now does not dictate but requests the wife to do a task for him. She is now emancipated, not a slave of the man. She is no longer the drudge and slave of olden days. She can divorce her husband, just as the husband can divorce her. She can sue the husband for her rights and can likewise be sued. The rigidity that was traditionally associated with sexual relationships no longer characterises the modern family. The woman in a modern family has attained an increasing degree of economic independence. It is not only the husband who leaves the home for work but it is also the wife who goes out of doors for work. This economic independence has largely affected the attitude of the modern woman. Previously, she had no choice but to find a male partner who could marry her and support her economically. She now does not feel helpless before her man but settles matters with him on her own terms.

"When it comes to equality for women, I think my family has always been a modern one, from day one." Balji chuckles. "I encourage independence for women. I encouraged my wife to drive, and the day she got her driving license, I felt liberated … Now, she is not dependent on me. Wherever she wants to go, she hops into the car and drives off. It was the single most liberating move she made. In the Middle East, the freer countries are the ones that allow women to drive."

So, what kind of family is the Balji family?

"A mixture. It is both traditional and modern."

Arrian and Roman

One is at an age where everything is interesting and worthy of comment, the other is dismissive and stays noncommittally cool. The difference between a happy eight-year-old and a chilled 12-year-old in a room is getting to hear the younger boy while the other tries to stay above it all. When I ask eight-year-old Roman what family means to him, he says family is his world, "Family is important because everyone in my family loves me … they care … they are kind." His little voice is accompanied by a broad white-toothed smile. He goes on to name everyone in his family, from his parents, brother to grandparents and great-grandmother in India. (When he mentions his brother, he says "especially my brother".)

"Family, especially your parents, are also strict," Balji interjects. "They are the ones who will punish you." He looks at his daughter, Deepa, sitting across the room.

Arrian adds, "He's got it three times today!" Arrian's body language is protective, even as he looks on with mock teen boredom. For a teenager who will turn 13 in a couple of days, Arrian sees himself as mature enough to carry the entire extended family's problems on his slender shoulders; from a need to "discipline" his kid brother, to his parents' work-life balance to his grandparents' security and health. Then there are the neighbours, some of whom he thinks are unfriendly, and a dog that belongs to his grandparents' neighbour. "I enjoy walking the dog even though she doesn't belong to me. Walking a dog is a good way of relieving stress. I think families should have a dog. Instead of fighting with one another, they can channel their energies to the pet. It's a pity we don't have one because there is a possibility the dog may jump off the balcony."

I make a mental note, both boys speak in full sentences and have an effortless grasp of the English language. It helps when your grandpa is a journalist, your father is a TV anchor and mother a former TV correspondent.

"I've made our special tea for you," Deepa places it on the glass table next to me. "This biscuit we made for Deepavali." The aroma from the tea is strong, with an agreeable spicy scent that reminds me of an Indian restaurant Balji took me to on Serangoon Road.

Unlike his younger brother, Arrian does not need to tell me

he loves his family; he expresses love through what he says about his family members and what he does. For example, he has a unique analogy for family: "Family is like a kettle," he says with his arms in the air, hands holding an imaginary kettle. "When it's turned on, it will boil, in two or perhaps three minutes. Family is the same, they make you angry and your blood boils. But they will find a way to turn it off, just like the kettle. It will reach boiling point and turn off, then cools down."

The boy is intelligent, of course, but there is also youthful wisdom, empathy and individualism, a combination that is likely to see him grow up as a special adult, probably one that takes the less trodden path. His kettle analogy betrays a cognitive understanding of family ties which goes beyond agile imagination, there is already a knowing of what the family unit can do and will endure.

"Your grandpa uses two words, wings and roots, for family," I look at Arrian and he nods. "Wings to fly out and explore the world, roots to come back when you encounter problems. The family is a place of calm and solace."

"I know his analogy," Arrian says with a smile in his voice. "My kettle analogy is better." His teenage conceit notwithstanding, it *is* better because his young mind already foresees and makes allowances for friction and discord within the family.

"Good analogy," says Balji, with pride in his voice. "I have not heard this one from you before."

Deepa smiles, "Yes, good analogy."

Moving the conversation along, I decide to steer away from family and probe into the emotional side of the boys. Looking at the younger boy, I ask, "Describe happiness. When was the happiest moment in your life?"

Roman's face brightens. "When I was given Winne the Pooh bear," he says, tentatively looking at his brother. "Arrian, you were happiest the day I was born."

Arrian does not want to respond, even though it is obvious he has said it for his brother to remember and repeat.

"When were you the happiest, Arrian?" I ask.

He turns to me, "When we all stayed together at Capella Hotel in Sentosa as a family. Both my grandparents came with us. And we are all going back again, at the end of the year." Arrian has brought the conversation back to family. Contrary to my understanding of teenagers, this young man has family foremost in his mind. "You are coming with us?" he looks at Balji.

"If I don't go to Kerala," Balji teases.

"Covid, it's not safe to travel out of the country," the boy is adamant about safety and looking forward to repeating the Capella experience in Sentosa. It is refreshing and reassuring that family is so important to a teenager.

"It's been arranged and confirmed," Deepa looks me in the eye. "It is a wonderful property, Capella. We had such a good time bonding as a family."

Roman looks at the watch on his tiny wrist, "My Chinese tuition starts at 3pm."

"It's only 2.30," Deepa assures her younger son. "We still have half an hour." She turns to me, "Throughout his entire time with the Chinese tutor, he speaks in Chinese. Arrian takes Malay and now French."

I am surprised and impressed.

With half an hour left, I decide to bring the focus to 27 Clover Way – why is it so special to them?

"Because Grandpa and Grandma live there," Roman says

simply without batting an eyelid. "I like to be with Grandpa and Grandma."

"It's calmer there," Arrian chips in. "And I like to walk the neighbour's dog. Oh, and there is a pot of bougainvillea. For six months it didn't flower. I talked to it, watered it. Now it is blossoming, with red, orange and yellow flowers."

Balji turns to me and says, "True, it's beautiful." I finish my tea and the Deepavali biscuit. "I'll give you a ride home," Balji says with a familiar wave of his right hand. As I turn to look at the two boys, I imagine them with wings, flying in their brave new world. With these two, they have strong roots and will never be far from home. I am reminded of the kettle – even when it boils, it will settle and calm down. Cool.

Before I step out of the apartment, I ask for a photo with the boys. Arrian takes my mobile and does something to the settings. He hands my mobile to his mother and asks me to pose with him and his brother.

"Look," he returns my mobile. The backdrop of the photo is dark, putting the focus on the three of us. It is such a happy photo, I like it. "When you write about us," his face sports a playful grin, "make sure I come across well."

Tai Ho with Arrian and Roman.

Chapter 7

He's Got Your Back

No manage-up culture with him as boss

What would Balji say?

"For someone who was a reporter, who knew her way around this country, I'm really bad now!" Irene Hoe's text message appears suddenly on my phone. She is obviously having difficulty figuring out where my apartment is. Then suddenly, "Am a tad early, I am downstairs."

"Come up." I am glad to be ready for her, questions bubbling in my head. Irene Hoe is a veteran journalist, and someone whom Balji thinks knows him "inside out". With more than 40 years' media experience under her belt, she is a writer, editor, coach and editorial consultant today.

"Even today, when I am given a story, this is how I begin channelling my thought process, 'What would Balji say?' I ask myself. It does not mean I would follow what he prescribes, but the process of listening to a suggestion, following up with that thought, and then coming up with my own approach," her eyes search, looking around my apartment, then stops, as if she has just stumbled on another thought. "It is the journalistic exercise I was used to in the newsroom with Balji. The curious and unrelenting intellectual exchanges that resulted in an approach to a story, and that was how good stories were hatched."

Irene Hoe is about Balji's age, early 70s, and like most journalists who have worked with Balji, she feels strongly that he occupies a unique place in Singapore journalism. *The Straits Times* has produced eminent editors like Peter Lim, Cheong Yip Seng, Leslie Fong and Han Fook Kwang. *The Business Times* has been edited by big name personalities like Mano Sabnani and Patrick Daniel. Warren Fernandez, the current editor-in-chief of *The Straits Times* (and Group Editor), has degrees from Oxford and Harvard. But Balji alone has the sole distinction of being involved in the launch of two daily newspapers in Singapore. Starting as the deputy editor of *The New Paper* when it debuted in 1988, he soon succeeded Peter Lim as editor and edited the paper for a decade, making it a successful, popular daily before going on to launch *TODAY* in 2000 for MediaCorp. And to top it all, he achieved these without a university degree.

"In all my years in the newspaper business, and there were many years, I learned the most from two bosses," says Irene, her voice thick and low. "Tan Wang Joo of *The Sunday Times*, and PN Balji, first from *The Straits Times* news desk and later, *The New Paper*. And between these two, what I learned from Balji went beyond learning how to pursue a story, tackle a story, write a story and edit a story. I had a ringside seat witnessing a leader and how, in his introverted and quiet way, he motivated his team."

She has a retentive memory and a knack for adding colourful asides, her innovative storytelling makes even the mundane sizzle. I put it to her years of journalistic training and working for a tabloid like *The New Paper*. I do not need to prompt her – like a reliable, pent-up rifle, she unleashes with relish when given the opportunity to fire freely. My Thursday with this news veteran is turning out to be an arresting and storied afternoon.

She hasn't moved an inch since she sat down opposite me in my living room, and refuses coffee, tea and wine. "They'll wreak havoc with my meds," she explains. "Perhaps Diet Coke, if you have it," her eyes look wicked, her face grimaces.

"I do. Coke without sugar?"

"That will do," her face breaks into a beam. "I prefer that."

"From all the people I have spoken to for this book, there is high regard and respect for Balji, the editor," I pause, then decide to start the afternoon with a provocation, a mixed comment from a former colleague of theirs. "Everyone agrees he was the best. Some did not take to his style. Agatha Koh, who worked with Balji at various times, thought he was intense and aloof. Let me quote her, 'A darn good editor, the best of the rest. Sharp, able to get to the point of anything. Didn't have much time for fluff (but he understood at times, some fluff was needed). Didn't go down so well with me as a manager … didn't fully explain some of his actions. His prerogative, I guess, but it didn't go down well for building trust. And not everyone trusted him. Overall, he was serious, rather intense but aloof. He was, still is, enigmatic.'"

Irene smiles, then nods, her way of saying she understands where that came from, then takes in a gulp of air, "I prefer not to comment on style. We all know Balji was not like the rest, which was why I appreciated him. He brought out the best in me. Even as the boss, the editor, he never stopped being a journalist," she catches her breath. "He could be in the streets, in the canteen or with his grandsons, he is always talking to strangers, eavesdropping, asking questions. Balji's mind never stops. I say, of all the senior editors, he was more or less the only 24-hour editor. When he was in the office, he was in the office; when he was not in the office, he was still in the office."

"Is that good?" I am not sure if the 24-hour editor description is a compliment or an insult in the contemporary workplace.

"Good and bad," she says, pursing her lips. "Unlike *The Straits Times* which is a huge ship compared to *The New Paper*, a small boat, the editor needs a comprehensive understanding of the entire operations including, crucially, a full understanding of the people working for him. In the case of *The Straits Times*, it is impossible for the editor to put his signature stamp on the paper, but in a smaller paper, Balji's signature stamp was undeniable. And to the journalists in the newsroom, his became the ultimate standard. You can't put anything past him. If it's a mistake, he'll catch it; if he likes what you have, the story would just get better. For a journalist, there is no greater encouragement than a boss who is also a journalist and has your back every step of the way." Again, she catches her breath, then continues, "Bad because he didn't have time for much else."

My mind suddenly remembers the Toh Chin Chye episode, a story that went horribly wrong, resulting in one journalist getting the sack and two senior editors getting demoted. (Further details of that episode later in this chapter.)

She reads my face and guesses what has just crossed my mind. "When the Toh Chin Chye incident happened, I was already out of *The New Paper*, and I had only one question, was Balji around? Of course, the answer was 'no'. He was on a pilgrimage to a mountain temple in Kerala, India. Even then, he rushed back and was fully involved in the aftermath. Any other editor would have been careful, making sure they were in no way contaminated by the toxic fallout."

"You said what you learned from Balji went beyond work,"

I need more on Balji the man. The journalist has been covered well in his own book, *Reluctant Editor*.

"After work, I could sit with Wang Joo for two hours, talking …" Irene slows down and starts to choose her words carefully. "She was strict and a straight talker, good was good, bad was not good – you damn well do it all over again. I learned a lot from that. With Balji, the learning was different. He was strict without being nasty and there was none of that macho bravado so common among the other male editors." She stops and drinks her Coke, buying time.

"He was close to me without me having to suck up to him … that was good for me. He gave me many important breaks in my career and I have to say they were all attributed to work and how I could get things done. I didn't need to suck up to him, and life was just so much easier. But what I observed was also that he himself did not kiss up to his bosses, whether it was to Peter, Cheong, Leslie or the all-important board. He got to where he was because of work, and that set a clean and simple example for us. Many of the editors played golf, sailed or were involved in activities that got them closer to the top. For Balji, family was important, and we admired his dedication to his wife and family. When he chose to be with his family or wife, we admired that, we respected it. When our boss has a life, we have a life. With Balji as boss, there was no manage-up culture."

There is something else lurking behind those bespectacled eyes, I can tell she is deep-diving into the ocean, the ocean of her many years in SPH. "Perhaps it is his special relationship with the women in his life, his wife and two daughters; or his quiet disposition. There was no implicit or explicit show of macho dominance. As a woman journalist, that was important. Those *New Paper* years were decades ago, but if you ask anyone today about *The New Paper*, the editor who comes to mind is Balji. Despite his soft and quiet self, his important family time and his lack of corporate savvy, the imprint he left on the paper was not something anyone could replicate."

*****

Now that Irene Hoe is familiar with my apartment, she manages to convince a former admin staff at *The New Paper*, Zainah Omar, to talk to me about Balji. "She is rank and file," Irene says in her deadpan voice. "She worked with Balji from 1988 to 2000. You will get a feel of what kind of man Balji is by talking to her, as she is a voice from the floor, so to speak."

Zainah recollects, "I was from admin, and my department coordinated everything: scheduling, housekeeping, computer issues, assets – everything. We were a crucial service." Zainah was with SPH for several decades, from 1980 to 2021, but there is still a girlish wonder in her voice when she revisits her days at *The New Paper*. In my living room, seated next to Irene Hoe, she says she wants to tell me the good *and* the bad about her former boss.

"Balji was a boss but also a friend, lah. Over the years, he got to know my husband and my family. He never asked about my family, but when I felt the need to talk, his door was always open and he listened. Working with Balji, over time, it was the human side that came first. I felt he cared for the support staff, the non-journalists. His secretary, the office assistants, admin assistants … For instance, Mala is an OA. He would ask her if she understood the page one headline.

If she understood it, then most Singaporeans would, too. He also encouraged us to come up with story ideas. By bringing us into the editorial team that way, we felt 'included', much more like a part of the whole newspaper. So even among the non-journalists, we felt our careers were also being developed. And I would say, that was what made the newsroom of *The New Paper* different."

So, we have the good, what about the bad?

"It was my duty to spot errors, and one day I spotted an error before publication, a pretty significant one," Zainah's eyes open wide. "I went to Balji and told him of the error. He shouted at me and scolded me. 'Go tell someone else!' This took place in the Production Department, and I felt the entire Production floor staring at me; I was so embarrassed. The man got his moods, lah."

Zainah takes out a file from her bag. "I printed out and kept messages regarding my service on *The New Paper*. When I need cheering up, I take them out and read them." She pushes a printout of a message towards me. "Later that day, he apologised," her right hand covers her mouth, her eyes dancing with excitement. "This was his message to me. 'I was rude this morning. Sorry. Your interventions are still welcome. I hope you won't react and say, "It's not even my job and this fella is so angry with me. Next time I wouldn't bother." I know you won't.'"

By now, Zainah's eyes are slightly misty. I can see why these messages are important, they bring back the real human interactions in ways that no official recognition can substitute. She picks another printout and reads it: "You are one of the big reasons that make me want to continue to edit TNP. Your work attitude, your commitment, your knowledge of TNP philosophy, are all exemplary. By the way, this is not a joke."

Later, when Zainah felt stressed out by work and decided to leave, she sent Balji a "by the way, this is not a joke" message herself, informing him that she had decided to resign. He shot back: "I read your message, hold on. I will tell you when to leave. Something big coming up very soon. After that, then you and I can leave together and start rumours about us. How about that?"

She didn't leave.

Drama in Tokyo

It's the fourth day of the athletics programme at the Tokyo Olympics, and halfway through the Games. The weekend brought dramatic developments not just in the track and field events, but also in table tennis (when the Singaporean players were eliminated), gymnastics (when China did not win all the events) and swimming (when the Chinese broke the dominance of the US and Australia to break a world record).

I am waiting for Balji in my apartment and watching the Olympics on TV, it's the heats of the women's 1500 metres event. The running commentary focuses on an Ethiopian-born runner representing The Netherlands, Sifan Hassan. The Dutch athlete is bidding for a hat-trick, it seems, with the 1500m, 5000m and 10,000m in her sight. She has the final of the 5000m later in the day. With the top six to qualify, the ideal scenario is to cruise through the race and conserve energy for the 5000m.

The race starts and she seems content to be trailing from behind. At the last lap, the bell rings, signalling only 400m to go. Hassan accelerates, each stride wider and stronger. Then suddenly, there is a tangle of legs in front of her, and Hassan has nowhere to go. She crashes into another competitor and crashes onto the running track. My coffee spills and my heart misses a beat. There goes the gold medal, what a waste!

Before my eyes (and the millions watching on TV), she picks herself up, and with only 200m left, starts to finish the race as if nothing has happened. She passes runner after runner and gets to the shoulders of the leaders at the top of the home straight. While she is able to ease off the pace, she still makes a statement by finishing first in a time of 4:05:17. It remains to be seen what impact this will have on her 5000m final later.

My heart is racing when Balji arrives. Next to politics, sports and the politics of sports consume him. *The New Paper* became what it did because of sports, or its unusual treatment of sports. If he was still an editor today, the Olympics and how to treat each story would have taken up his days and nights. But he is still a journalist today when it comes to each story and how they are treated by the press. And there is one hot story about the Olympics that is of particular interest to him – the astonishing rise and dramatic fall of Singapore Olympic gold medalist, Joseph Schooling.

The drama was almost as high as Sifan Hassan's, except it was just the opposite, there was no accident and it ended shockingly bad. While Hassan stirred up wonder and admiration, Schooling prompted online mockery. The swimmer who won Singapore's first and only Olympics gold medal thus far – five years ago in Rio de Janeiro – failed to qualify in the same event in Tokyo, for the 100m butterfly. And to add salt to injury, he finished last in his qualifying heat.

Days before the race, the media had primed the entire country into a mild state of frenzy, reminding its citizens of his sensational victory in Rio, playing back the winning race again and again. He did not just win, the media reminded Singaporeans, he beat American swimmer Michael Phelps, the most successful and most decorated Olympian of all time, in an Olympic record.

In lane eight, closest to the camera, Schooling appeared overweight as he assumed his position before the race. It was his fifth heat. He was slow off the blocks and by the time he somersaulted into the home stretch, he was trailing way behind. He clocked 53.12 seconds, and was placed 44th out of the field of 55. His time was almost three seconds slower than the 50.39 seconds that helped him win the gold at Rio. Talking to CNA shortly after, the swimmer said, "It's a very disappointing performance overall, but there's always another one. It's not going to end like this."

Shocked, most Singaporeans could not believe that their champion could sink so low, not even entering the semi-finals and coming last in his heat. Many could not refrain from expressing themselves on social media and, of course, some went overboard. Keyboard warriors were out in full force, hurling all sorts of invectives. "Still number one, but from behind." "Too much Milo."

"I did not want to watch the Schooling race," Balji says emphatically. "I knew he was going to lose, but I just didn't expect him to come in last in his heat. To some extent, most Singaporeans were initially shamed, they didn't expect the champion to sink this low. And for that, we have the media to blame."

If the public and media had tracked Schooling's performances and timings over the past four years after the

Rio Games, they would have seen this coming. "It is the job of the media not only to track but also to inform. For instance, at the World Championships in 2017, an American, Caeleb Dressel, clocked 49.86 seconds in the 100m butterfly final. Kristof Milak came in second, in 50.62 seconds. Schooling was third in 50.83 seconds. That was the first sign that all was not right." I can tell, if he had still been in charge of a media outlet, this would have been highlighted before Tokyo.

And since then, Schooling's times have been regressing. At the 2018 Asian Games, he won the gold in 51.04 seconds. At the 2019 FINA World Championships, he clocked 52.93 seconds in the heats and didn't qualify for the semi-finals. He was 24th out of 77 swimmers. "Did the media raise the alarm? No," says Balji, shaking his head. "They probably didn't want to play the bad cop, but they should have sounded the alarm prominently and asked the question, 'Can our Olympic champion defend his title in the next Olympics?' It would have been unpopular, but it was the responsible thing to do."

But in 2021, at the ISCA International Senior Cup in Florida in March, Schooling clocked 52.93 seconds again, to finish second behind Dressel, who cruised in at 51.69 seconds. "It was clear then, as we approached the Olympics, that Schooling wasn't going to win a medal, much less successfully defend his title. The sports officials knew it too, but no one wanted to be the one to raise the red flag. They made noises here and there. Nothing else. And so, Singapore happily coasted into the Tokyo Games and you can't blame the public for expecting something when the media irresponsibly flagged him out to be the man to watch."

And there is something else. Balji's eyes shift and I know he is finding the most accurate way to say what's on his mind.

"The family," he starts. "The Schoolings were too close to the media, so much so that the Schooling family was named 'The Straits Times Singaporean of the Year' in 2016. This win was decided after a public vote and deliberated by a 15-judge panel. They called May Schooling 'auntie' and Colin 'uncle'. Is this healthy?"

Why not?

"If the relationship is so intimate, how can the media be objective when they cover anything on the Schoolings?" His question is both curious and exasperated. "I don't blame the family, I blame the media. The media was milking and extending the shelf life of a champion way past its expiry date."

More important for Balji was the back story of the Olympics, one which most Singaporeans are not conscious of. He suggests looking behind the journey to Rio, a journey that was a decidedly lonely one, one that the family took upon themselves, with little or no real support from anyone, especially from the swimming fraternity. "Most people have the mistaken notion that our Olympic athletes are completely funded by the state. In fact, the opposite is the case," he tries not to sound vexed.

"Right from the start, when Joseph Schooling went to study overseas at a school known for its academic and sporting excellence to nurture his Olympic dreams, all expenses were borne by his parents, Colin and May. They also paid for specialist coaches and trips to various competitions. They drew on their reserves. They sold their property in Australia and ended part of their insurance endowment plan to finance their son's journey to become a champion. Only when Schooling started to make waves in the swimming circuits in the US, just before he turned professional, did the government money come in, late in the game. By the time money came from the Singapore government, Schooling had already made a name for himself internationally, and was able to get scholarships, such as the one from the University of Texas."

From as early as the 1970s, when Junie Sng won gold medals in the SEA Games and Asian Games, it has always been the commitment of the families, not the government, that resulted in champions for Singapore. "For the Schoolings, Colin and May made the tough call to send their son to Austin, Texas, halfway around the world in 2009 because they knew it was the only way, the only environment their son needed to be in, to even have a chance at an Olympic medal. All in, they invested $1.35m of their own money to fulfill their son's dream. Husband and wife took turns shuttling between Singapore and the US to take care of their young son, each staying for months at a time."

They wanted to learn about all aspects of swimming, especially the technical aspects. So, they built an extensive swim library at home, took the swimming association officials' credentials tests, attended many courses and lectures conducted by experts, served as honorary treasurers in the swimming associations for two years. They played hosts to many visiting Olympic swim teams from the US, Canada, Australia, Switzerland, France and Italy.

When Colin Schooling passed away on 18 November 2021, Balji wrote "In Death, Schooling Leaves Behind a Gift for Fathers" in *The New Singapore*, where he recounted a father's obsession, how he prepared meticulously and doggedly to crack Singapore's toughest nut, Mindef, to obtain NS deferment for his son:[1]

"Nearly every local and international event Joseph took part in was documented. May and I would have our worksheets ready to monitor his reaction times off the block, split times, stroke counts and strikes rates. We did this so that we could be constructive in our opinions and advice to our son. We could not just rely on his coaches totally because they were busy with others under their charge," Colin said.

Not to forget the swimming aids like tailor-made goggles and a drag chute attached to the waist to build the swimmer's strength and endurance through resistance. Nothing was left to chance. Everything was planned to precision and recorded.

Armed with all the details, the parents presented their voluminous report to Mindef. It was difficult for Mindef to say no and thus Joseph became the first youth to get deferment.

"It was the first deferment they granted. One can imagine the amount of bureaucratic red tape involved, the amount of information they needed to provide. So, if you ask me who we need to thank, apart from Joseph Schooling himself, who else deserves our gratitude, it must be the parents, no one else really."

They did it once, and they achieved their goal. For subsequent Olympics, shouldn't the sports fraternity have taken over? "I still remember when the National Stadium was built, Lee Kuan Yew said it would be a white elephant. We are not a sporting country, there is no sporting culture here. Once in four years, the public gets interested and starts shooting from the hip: Where is the gold? Why no medal? Why so bad?"

As John F. Kennedy once said, "Victory has a thousand fathers, but defeat is an orphan."

Unlike the US, China and many European countries where there is a proper state programme to guide each athlete from a tender age, the journey to an Olympic gold is a long and torturous one in Singapore. There is no precedent for gold, there is definitely no precedent for a gold medalist to defend his title. "Some quarters argue that Singapore is too small," Balji laughs. "Really? There are smaller and poorer countries. Yet they have run, swum and out-performed bigger and richer countries. New Zealand has five million people, smaller than Singapore's population, yet claimed seven golds, six silvers and seven bronzes to finish 13th on the medal table at the Tokyo Olympics. Jamaica got both gold and silver for the 100m dash. Bahamas, Puerto Rico and Morocco have also clinched gold. What I find really curious is why big businesses have not come in and made an effort. Adopt an athlete with potential, for example; they can afford it."

Mentally, I see Sifan Hassan sprinting at the end of the 10,000m to her third medal and second gold. Born in Ethiopia but moved to The Netherlands at the age of 15, hers is a success story, from Third World adversity to First World victory. There are both state and club money to see her through. I share Balji's frustration, Singapore should relook its whole sports ecosystem. "We can be less opportunistic and more strategic," is his parting comment.

When an athlete represents his country, the country should have his back, all the way.

We have a problem

To a huge audience at the launch of the crisis management book, *We Have a Problem* (see Chapter 4), Balji described the Toh Chin Chye episode as "the worst crisis that can happen to a newspaper ... one of the saddest moments in my journalism career, and one of the worst things that can happen to a journalist."

Recounting it now in my living room 25 years later, every detail is still alive, every remark sounds loud and piercing and the sequence of events still cascades down painfully. "It is a story that gets relived again and again in my mind, which is why I remember it so clearly," his voice dry, the anguish still haunts. "It must have been divine intervention. I was in India when it happened. Would it have happened if I was around in the newsroom? Most likely. The circumstances were so ripe for a disaster like that to happen, and I have said it before, it was a disaster waiting to happen at *The New Paper*."

This was how it was subsequently reported by UPI:[2]

Singapore newspaper offers damage pay

Singapore, Jan. 23 1996 – A Singapore tabloid newspaper Tuesday publicly offered to pay damages after wrongly reporting a former high-ranking government minister had been arrested in connection with a fatal hit-and-run car accident. *The New Paper* Saturday had reported former Deputy Prime Minister Toh Chin Chye, 74, was arrested, when the real suspect was a 33-year-old salesman bearing the same name. A 17-year-old student died in the accident.

The elder Toh was a founding chairman of the People's Action Party, which has dominated Singapore politics

since 1959. On Saturday, the tabloid's front page
carried the headline 'Hit-and-run accident case:
Ex-DPM Toh Chin Chye arrested', along with a
photograph of the former senior official. The article, on
page 6, also carried Toh's picture.

'We have agreed to pay Dr Toh damages and to
indemnify him for all legal costs incurred', *The New
Paper* said in an apology notice published on the
front page of Tuesday's *Straits Times*, Singapore's
leading newspaper. The notice was attributed to the
reporter who wrote the erroneous article, along with
The New Paper's editor and publisher, Singapore Press
Holdings, which owns all of the nation's newspapers.
'We would also like to apologise to all Singaporeans for
besmirching the name of one of our founding fathers,'
the notice read. …

A Singapore media source, who asked not to be named,
said the reporter who wrote the article was acting on a
tip and did not know he was writing about the wrong
Toh Chin Chye. 'Given the circumstances and details
of the accident, *The New Paper* should have realised
that Dr Toh could not have been the person involved
and should have investigated the matter further,' the
published apology said. Several foreign publications
in the past year have been ordered to pay hundreds
of thousands of dollars in damages after defaming
Singapore leaders and questioning the relationship
between the nation's government and its judiciary.

But why does Balji insist that even if he was around, it
might have still happened?

Balji's assessment of the situation was shared during the book launch event in 2016 and reported in an article by Robin Hicks:[3]

> "How did it happen? Because the reporter – who was an extremely good crime reporter – had a source in traffic police, and that source had always been right … except for this time."

> "I remember talking to the reporter and he told me that he went back to check with the Sergeant [and asked] 'Is it the DPM?' And the Sergeant said 'yes'."

> "There were three standard operating procedures that were not followed," Balji explained, "One … you must get an official spokesman to confirm or deny [the story] or give a comment. But the journalist was so sure of his source."

> "The second is, *The New Paper* is an afternoon paper. There was the fear that if he [the reporter] goes to the police spokesman, the spokesman might leak it to other papers and he'd lose the story." …

> The third risk the paper took was to avoid putting the story in SPH's publishing schedule for fear others would run with it.

> "The schedule goes to the [SPH] editor-in-chief, who would I'm sure have asked: 'Toh Chin Chye? It cannot be. Hit and run? It cannot be. Driving a panel van? It cannot be.' But he didn't see the schedule," Balji recalled, …

And there was something else that Balji sees as the "Fatal Distraction": "A last-minute statement from the Prime Minister's Office, about Lee Kuan Yew being admitted to the hospital with chest pains – it sent the newsroom into a storm of frenzy. And in the whole rush and madness, the Toh Chin Chye story did not get the attention it would otherwise have had. That's why I say it was like a perfect storm."

When Balji was writing *Reluctant Editor*, and former *New Paper* colleagues knew he was gathering information to write a chapter on the Toh Chin Chye affair, almost everyone was against it, especially those directly involved in it, the journalist who got sacked and editors who were demoted. Two decades had passed, why bring it up now, they asked.

Yaw Yan Chong knows me. "Ex MediaCorp? I remember you," he says in his response to my text message.

"I have a favour to ask," I begin.

"Sure, what's up?"

"I am writing a book on Balji and the episode of *The New Paper* came up. The Toh Chin Chye episode. I hope it is okay to revisit this."

His response is what I had expected, but I needed to ask anyway. "To be honest," he texts, "it's something that I do not want to revisit. Said the same thing to Balji when he asked for the same thing. Let the past stay in the past."

I try from another angle. "I just want to know how you feel about the way they resolved it. Was it fair?"

"I honestly don't think about it anymore." Yan Chong keeps it casual. When I apologise for disturbing him, he quips, "No worries." He works for Reuters now, and is doing well.

How *The New Paper* bounced back from the spectre of the Toh Chin Chye affair has been well documented in Balji's book, *Reluctant Editor*. Now in my living room, Balji has a few more things to say.

"I don't miss the newsroom," he starts, a look of resolve on his face. "People don't believe me when I tell them that. I am still keenly curious and interested in news, especially local news, politics, economic and social trends; I follow them with the zest of a young journalist. Occasionally, I write for publications when I feel like it, but even when I don't, I still have my network, still check and counter-check sources when I read the headlines and other stories."

You can take the journalist out of a newsroom, but you cannot take the newsroom out of the journalist. He doesn't miss the newsroom? Who is he kidding?

"When you have survived a crisis like the Toh Chin Chye episode, and live to write about it, successfully launched underdog papers, helped relaunch publications overseas, I have achieved almost everything. There is nothing left to prove. So today, I am just thankful that my mind still functions as a journalist, always asking questions, always curious."

It's three in the afternoon and the sun casts a golden glow over the skyline. Balji has been to my apartment many times before, but it's the first time he is witnessing a golden skyline, from the 21st floor. This is the perfect time for Balji to be retrospective, take stock and perhaps assess the successes and failures of his life as a newspaper man.

"Most, if not all your former colleagues, hail you as one of the best editors they have worked with. You were a full-time journalist even when you were an editor and brought out the best in them. Some also saw you as intense, aloof, even cynical. Your silent and independent streaks did not engender trust. How does it feel to hear these comments?"

"Ha ha ha, you don't know how good it makes me feel to hear the truth. I am not god. I like to hear the good, the not so good and the very ugly. It makes me human." It is clear he gets a kick hearing how he was regarded but it is also clear that nothing bothers him too much at 72.

"I agree, I can be aloof, and in the newsroom, I didn't always have time to explain myself. But I must add, a measure of cynicism is a healthy thing in a journalist. A journalist or an editor shouldn't trust too easily. The Toh Chin Chye incident wouldn't have happened if there was enough cynicism.

"I am happy to hear what my former colleagues say about my editorship. I had a good ride. If you asked me to be the editor of *The Straits Times*, I would decline. It's too big a ship to manoeuvre. I won't be as effective. It is like a tanker, a ship, but I am used to a sampan, a small boat. I want to know everything, every staff, the paper has to have my imprint as editor. This is not possible in a big broadsheet like *The Straits Times*, only possible with smaller dailies like *TODAY* and *The New Paper*. And I am particularly good when a daily is under siege, is an underdog needing to prove itself. Both *TODAY* and *The New Paper* were underdogs in their days, we had to carve out our niche for ourselves, build the readership from zero, build a credible database and knock on every advertiser's door. That was what I was good at."

Editor of *The Straits Times*, not everyone gets that honour. So, again, if given the job, would he have taken it on? Balji dismisses it again, "That won't happen, so it's academic."

Why?

"Top SPH management may acknowledge my ability to generate good political stories," he says with a shrug of his shoulders. "But I don't think they have too much trust in my ability with economic stories, or stories on foreign policy. It's a pity, I would have proven them wrong. Anyhow, it's moot."

What kind of editor was he? How would he describe himself?

"When I was made the editor of *The New Paper* and later *TODAY*, I did not set out to fit into any mould," his voice thoughtful and reflective. "I was just going to be me. A bit like Goh Chok Tong when he became PM. He knew he wasn't Lee Kuan Yew; he wasn't going to change to be more like LKY, it wouldn't be him. It's the same with me. I can't and won't pretend to be anyone else." No golf, tennis, squash or sailing, none of the activities that would gather corporate management together and talk shop. Or in Irene Hoe's words, none of that "macho bravado" widely on display. Instead, he was the quiet one in the corner or in the back row, who rarely spoke in a group and as someone pointed out, the editor and CEO with shoes but no socks. When the board members wanted to see or talk to him, they would ask him to their office during office hours.

Group CEO of MediaCorp, Ernest Wong, got a taste of Balji's independence when the former decided to call him on a Saturday. Balji was on his way to watch a football match, and when he realised it was a trivial matter, did not hide his displeasure. "Ernest, you called me on a Saturday for this? Can't it wait till Monday?"

It was clear, over time, that the "Balji approach" to work was professional in the strictest sense of the word. He had always known Peter Lim, but because of their professional relationship, never became friends with him. "Peter only became a good friend when he left SPH," he reminds me. "I started inviting him to my home and social functions, but before that, I didn't feel it was right."

This "proper" approach towards work allowed him a high degree of independence. In his journalistic world of news, it was needed. "I based all my judgement calls on journalistic merits, no favours, no owing this person or paying back the other person. I even distrusted ministerial briefings. In *TODAY*, I asked Walter Fernandez to represent me most of the time during these ministerial briefings, unless it was absolutely crucial for me to attend."

But it didn't mean he was not practical. Following the fallout from the Toh Chin Chye episode, the recommendation from SPH management was to sack all three responsible, the journalist Yan Chong, the acting editor Ivan Fernandez and big desk editor Ken Jalleh Jr. To this day, most in the newsroom still feel that it was not right to sack only the reporter and demote the editors. But Balji's point was this: sack the editors and the paper would never be able to recover. In life, we make choices, and sometimes the best options aren't out there.

I hear Irene's voice here, once again. What's important — he's got your back.

NOTES

1   PN Balji, "In Death, Schooling Leaves Behind a Gift for Fathers", *The New Singapore*, 24 November 2021. Reproduced in the Annex of this book.

2   UPI, "Singapore newspaper offers damage pay", 23 January 1996; UPI Archives <https://www.upi.com/Archives/1996/01/23/Singapore-newspaper-offers-damage-pay/2281822373200/>.

3   Robin Hicks, "*The New Paper* Toh Chin Chye story blunder 'worst crisis that can happen to a newspaper' says former CEO P N Balji", *Mumbrella Asia*, 18 April 2016 <https://www.mumbrella.asia/2016/04/the-new-papers-toh-chin-chye-story-blunder-worst-crisis-that-can-happen-to-a-newspaper-says-former-ceo-p-n-balji>.

Chapter 8

Identity

Singapore's multiracialism: still a work in progress

A racial formula

3 September 2020, 9.30am: An Indian woman boarded bus service 182 from Tuas Checkpoint. Listening to music using her earphones, she noticed a woman pointing and staring at her. The woman ranted:

> Your heart is so black ... everything is black .... Stupid Indian ... you are an Indian, so black ... I hate your skin... I don't like your face.

The Indian woman recorded these abuses on her phone, then stood up and asked the other woman if there was anything wrong. The abuses continued, she called the police and informed the bus captain to stop the bus near Singapore Discovery Centre.[1]

*****

12 April 2021: A video clip showed a man ignoring a woman who continuously berated him in both English and Mandarin and accusing him of molesting her at Boon Lay MRT station:

> You are not my type, I am not your type. Full stop. Malay touching a Chinese, what is this? ... Boon Lay station has a lot of CCTVs [closed-circuit television] okay?

The woman, Tan Beow Hiong, 57, maintained a YouTube channel that had multiple videos alleging racism or harassment by persons of other races, including a video with the title "Malay Man Attempted to Molest Chinese Woman", in which she repeatedly insinuated that Malays should not be touching Chinese.

*****

7 May 2021, 8.30am: A 55-year-old private tutor, Hindocha Nita Vishnubhai, an Indian Singaporean, was brisk walking from Chua Chu Kang MRT station towards the stadium when she received racist verbal abuse and was physically attacked by a man, as reported in *The Straits Times*.[2] The victim of the attack made a police report and the matter was also raised in Parliament, prompting the Prime Minister to add in a post on his Facebook page, "I am very disappointed and seriously concerned that this racist attack could happen in Singapore."

*****

5 June 2021: Mr Tan Boon Lee, a 60-year-old senior lecturer at Ngee Ann Polytechnic's School of Engineering, was caught in a video confronting an interracial couple , telling them that it was a disgrace for a Chinese girl and an Indian man to be together.

Mr Dave Parkash, 26, was with his girlfriend, Ms Jacqueline Ho, 27, on Orchard Road when Mr Tan confronted him. He said it was not the first time he had experienced racism when he was out with Ms Ho. Throughout their seven-year relationship, there have been instances where people would look disapprovingly at them. He is of Indian and Filipino parentage, while his girlfriend is half-Thai and half-Chinese. Mr Parkash said he had uploaded the video on the Internet as he felt compelled to raise awareness that such racism still continues to exist in Singapore, though he had not expected the video to go viral.

*****

This case seems to be the last straw that broke the camel's back when it comes to racism. Suddenly, everyone has a view.

Opposition leader Pritam Singh said society should call out bigoted views, even if they are privately held. As reported in a 2021 *Mothership* article,[3] Singh said, "Bigoted views, even if privately held, have a nasty habit of showing themselves up opportunistically in day-to-day circumstances."

Law Minister K Shanmugam wrote about the incident on his Facebook page, stating that the increasing number of such incidents involving open racism was "quite unacceptable, very worrying … I used to believe that Singapore was moving in the right direction on racial tolerance and harmony. Based on recent events, I am not so sure anymore."

All these culminated in a policy speech by Lawrence Wong on 25 June 2021.[4] It is important for the majority community in Singapore to do its part and be sensitive to the needs of the minorities, he said. In a multiracial society anywhere in the world, it is harder to be a minority than a majority. "We must have the humility to acknowledge our multiracialism is still a work in progress, the honesty to recognise that not everyone will want to move at the same pace. And yet persevere to protect our multiracialism. Cherish it, nurture it, strengthen it."

When I raise the issue of racism with Balji, and have done so quite a few times before, it has always been greeted with a smile and a sigh. "My experience has been different," he quips. "Growing up, I have had my fair share of jokes about Indians. But they did not and do not upset me. I truly believe them to be jokes. There was an Indian character in an old TV comedy, 'Mind Your Language', who was the trigger of many stereotypical jokes about Indians. We all laughed, but we were not upset. Even watching the TV show today, I am not upset. What's important is that the scriptwriter did not mean it. The lines were meant to create laughter."

He turns to something more fundamental in this big topic of race. "The term 'racism' is often poorly understood," he says with both hands on the table. "The dictionary defines it as 'prejudice, discrimination, or antagonism directed against someone of a different race based on the belief that one's own race is superior'. These incidents that have happened in Singapore in the past two years are primarily aimed at one race, Indians. And they arose mainly as a result of CECA, also known as the Comprehensive Economic Cooperation Agreement."

CECA is a free trade agreement between Singapore and India to strengthen bilateral trade. It was signed on 29 June 2005. As reflected in a *Mothership* article,[5] the CECA has become a source of unhappiness for some Singaporeans who believe that the Indian professionals are stealing their jobs and are crowding out Singaporeans in their own society. Some also believe the government is allowing Indian professionals to achieve citizenry and eventually gain their vote for the ruling party. These worries have become more pronounced as Singapore battles its worst recession and countries around the world continue struggling to contain the Covid-19 pandemic.

"I blame the government on two fronts: one, for not explaining CECA clearly to the public; and two, for not being able to see the need in the economy for the type of skills needed. Singapore has lost out in the skills games," Balji's voice cracks a little. He continues, "Today, North Indians, highly educated, talented, make a lot of money because of the skills Singaporeans do not have. Yet Singaporeans have this mistaken notion that they are here to take away their jobs. The truth is, without them, the economy will suffer."

And he has one simple question for Pritam Singh, "How do you call out privately-held bigoted views? Perhaps what's more effective is to attack bigoted behaviour head on. If someone walks away from me because they think I don't smell good as an Indian, my response is, come closer, I smell very good. If they think I am dirty, I'll show them that I am cleaner. The idea is to break down the prejudice, episode by episode, one experience at a time. Find a way to say something that won't antagonise or cause suspicion. This is an issue that cannot be solved in a day, month or year. We are in this for the long haul."

There is one part of Lawrence Wong's speech that Balji agrees with. "It's idealistic, but what's wrong with idealism when it's the right course of action? S Rajaratnam pushed for the melting pot route, Lee Kuan Yew disagreed, so did Lee Hsien Loong. I am with Lee Kuan Yew and Lee Hsien Loong on this," says Balji.

In Lawrence Wong's speech of 25 June 2021, he had said:[6]

We did not set out to achieve racial harmony by creating a monolithic society. Our multi-racialism does not require any community to give up its heritage or traditions.

Ours is not the French way, insisting on assimilation into one master language and culture: Speak French, accept French ways and assimilate into French society. Instead we decided to preserve, protect and celebrate our diversity.

Hence, we encourage each community to take pride in its own cultures and traditions. At the same time, we seek common ground among our communities, and aim to expand our common space and strengthen our shared sense of belonging and identity.

...

This is our distinctive philosophy of multiracialism in Singapore. We do not devalue diversity, but we accept and celebrate it. Multi-racialism in Singapore doesn't mean forgetting our separate racial, linguistic, religious and cultural identities. It doesn't require us to erase our rich inheritances in favour of a bland and homogenised broth.

"It is idealistic," repeats Balji. "And it has its problems, but respecting one's roots goes a long way in building confidence and identity, and in turn respecting someone else's identity. It is only by knowing who you are that you respect and even honour someone else's identity. Both my daughters married men of Indian origin, without my wife and I interfering, one lives all the way in Canada. My younger daughter, Divya, married a Canadian of Indian origin. Deepa married a man of

Sri Lankan origin. They are confident adults with their own families and contributing to the country they live in."

A speech on race

The National Day Rally is an annual speech given by the Prime Minister of Singapore to the nation, traditionally on the first or second Sunday after 9 August, Singapore's National Day.[7] Since 1966, the rally has been an annual event through which the Prime Minister speaks directly to the citizens of Singapore on the country's achievements and also its key challenges, the state of the economy, policy changes and its plans for the future.[8]

As explained in a 2016 article in *The Straits Times*,[9] in 1966, a transcript of a "private meeting" between the Prime Minister and community leaders was released to the media two weeks after the event. It could be considered Singapore's first National Day Rally. It continued annually, and in 1971, Lee Kuan Yew decided "at the last minute" to televise the speech live; it has since been telecast live every year.

In 2021, the speech was delivered at MediaCorp, delayed until 29 August; there was no rally speech the year before because of Covid-19. Lee Hsien Loong decided to use 100-year-old Lim Tze Peng to illustrate how each race should take pride in his or her own rich cultural heritage. Race is emerging as an issue the Prime Minister can no longer ignore, and more and more, the issue of race is being coupled with the issue of foreign talent and jobs. Speaking in Mandarin, the Prime Minister says he met Mr Lim two months back, and was astounded by his spirit of continuous learning, even past a hundred years of age. "Over the years, he found his own language of expression, which is neither Eastern nor

Western, but Singaporean," says the Prime Minister.

"PM mentions Lim Tze Peng," Balji's text message appears. I feel somewhat honoured that the man I wrote a book on is mentioned by the Prime Minister. I know Balji watches the rally every year with a critical eye. The regional papers will come knocking for an analysis; almost every year he contributes an opinion piece to *Yahoo* and occasionally to CNN or the BBC when the rally touches on regional or international topics.

When Balji, on his way to a lunch appointment, stops by my apartment for a chat about the National Day Rally speech, he raises his concern that one area where racial issues require urgent attention is in the workplace, echoing the view he had expressed in a 2021 *Yahoo News* article,[10] "where Singaporeans have first-hand experience of how foreigners perform. And, generally speaking, it has not been a pretty sight."

Balji's view of the situation was clearly set out in the article:

The frustrations follow a similar pattern: many Singaporeans claim that foreigners have stolen our jobs, tend to mix with their own kind, are good at currying favour with the bosses, and so on. Some of these accusations are exaggerations but when repeated over lunch and coffee, they have a way of being believed.

He went on to point out the lack of government action:

[T]he government has not taken the bull by the horns, letting the issue simmer. An opportunity came after the 2011 general election when voters showed their anger at the sudden spike in foreign workers who, in their eyes, were responsible for jamming up transport and making flats harder to get.

Yet, the government did not address the angst directly, hoping that medical subsidies for the Pioneer Generation would do the trick to assuage voters. Ten years later, partly because of Covid, the frustrations are boiling over.

Our discussion turns to the government's reticence in this area and whether the issue of foreign talent and foreign labour is such a taboo subject. "Race and the issue of foreigners in our midst have always been tricky for the government. So, they wrapped it up into an economic argument," Balji says, shaking his head slightly. "They think the economic argument would be enough." As he noted in his article, the government "has been too focused on the economy" and with the fact that, given the "over-reliance on foreign labour, restricting the flow of outsiders would only force companies to look elsewhere to grow their pie."[11]

As Balji had elaborated in his article:

In fact, Lee did tell Singaporeans not to push too hard as trade and investments are the country's lifeblood. "We must not ... give the impression that Singapore is becoming xenophobic and hostile to foreigners. It would gravely damage our reputation as an international hub. It would cost us investments, jobs and opportunities," he said.

However, he feels that this approach is essentially "... using intellectual and ideological reasons to fight what are essentially emotional arguments. And from anecdotal evidence, this has not worked. The pandemic has silenced the government's arguments."

Balji has a side story to share in the article:

Just hours before Prime Minister Lee Hsien Loong spoke on race relations and wage disparity on Sunday (29 August), I had a rude awakening on how deep the race divide has seeped into our body politic. I have heard many stories about racial discrimination in Singapore but what this 12-year-old boy told his father at a cafe was not something I thought I would ever hear. "The lady gave me a plate of rice when I asked for fries. That is because I am an Indian," he said without batting an eyelid.

I was at a loss for words after hearing the comments. Meanwhile, his father kept silent, not wanting to engage his son on how he came to that conclusion. An opportunity was lost, I must say, to ask the boy what made him equate the lady's action to an issue of race.

And Balji maintains his position that racism in Singapore has been misunderstood or "misplaced", based more on "feel", less on facts. As noted in his article, "My gut feel, having spoken to many Singaporeans here, is that their experiences with what they call racism are somewhat misplaced." This is underscored by the fact that, as explained in his article, his queries as to what made one feel that he or she was the victim of a racist attack inevitably draws a response of "I can't prove it. But we felt that way."[12]

Somewhat misplaced, yet, as he said earlier, with repetition, misplaced assumptions have a way of being believed and emerging as urban truths. What should Singaporeans and the government do to prevent this from becoming a self-fulfilled prophecy?

As pointed out in Balji's article,[13] the Prime Minister has said "the government [will] take that elusive first step to make discrimination in the workplace *illegal* ... The guidelines for fair and progressive employment will soon be written into the law to deal with a problem that has been spilling over into the public space as after-effects of the Covid crisis." On this forthcoming enactment of new legislation, Balji says, "Implementing it decisively, squarely and fairly will make the difference in lessening the misperceptions about race among Singaporeans."

Some parts of the Prime Minister's speech bear repeating and emphasising:[14]

> The real solution to racism is to change social attitudes.
> Individual and social attitude. This takes time and
> effort. Legislation can play a role. Laws may not by
> themselves make people get along with one another or
> like one another. But laws can signal what our society
> considers right or wrong, and nudge people over time
> to behave better.
>
> ...
>
> We intend to pass specific legislation on Racial
> Harmony. We will call it The Maintenance of Racial
> Harmony Act. It will collect together in one place all
> the Government's powers to deal with racial issues.
> It will also incorporate some softer, gentler touches.
> For example, the power to order someone who has
> caused offence to stop doing it, and to make amends by

learning more about the other race and mending ties with them. ...

"I am glad they are finally doing this," says Balji with a grin. "Better late than never." On the new legislation announced by the Prime Minister, he remarks, "They have allowed the laws here to be flexible with a lot of room to manoeuvre. Like the Maintenance of Religious Harmony Act, if they enforce it well, there may also be no need to invoke the punishments under the new Act, as the Prime Minister has said of the Maintenance of Religious Harmony Act."[15]

Less and less Singaporean

"I came to Singapore at the ripe age of one." Born in India, Balji likes to describe Singapore as his adopted country. "I am in my 70s now, so I am older than independent Singapore. As a child, adult and now a senior, I am a witness to all of Singapore's milestones. I am thankful for what Singapore has done for me, and how, for better or worse, it has also influenced the sort of person I have become. Even without a university education, I have been relatively successful, and more importantly, have been able to raise my family here."

I can hear a *but* coming.

"But I have become less and less Singaporean," he says, his voice devoid of emotion.

"When I was fully employed, I was too engrossed with my work to notice anything. I am retired now and I have more time to look and observe. I have started to see how ungracious a society we have become. The political space is also changing in ways that affect me more than I had expected. I worked mostly over the years when two prime ministers ruled Singapore: Lee Kuan Yew and Goh Chok Tong. They affected the way I worked and lived. LKY was strong and decisive. Goh was different. He had to manoeuvre the tight space that LKY left for him. Both PMs contributed in their unique ways."

Balji has read *Tall Order: The Goh Chok Tong Story* by Peh Shing Huei. While Lee Kuan Yew's place in Singapore history is well and solidly placed, not enough, he feels, has been said about Goh. "When I joined *TODAY*, I took a few months to settle down and I was invited to lunch with Goh Chok Tong. I was waiting outside the small banquet room and was expecting the press secretary to come and fetch me. Instead, the Prime Minister himself appeared. 'Hi Balji, let's go in for lunch,' he said. That was year 2000, 21 years ago, but I remember it like it was yesterday. And the first question he asked me was, 'How is your brother?' He knew my brother was a national football coach at the height of the Malaysia Cup mania. Small things are sometimes the big things. Those two 'small' gestures really impressed me. He came across as a genuine person and I remember telling myself, I can relate to this man.

"As the Prime Minister after LKY, he decided to govern by consensus, by talking to as many people as possible, to build a collective view, building a consensus. His stated goal was to achieve a gentler society. That was a very brave thing to do after decades of the iron-fisted approach of LKY. To announce it openly to Singaporeans was tantamount to a policy reversal in the face of the most respected and feared man in Singapore's history. You have to be a very confident and brave man. Some Singaporeans thought he was weak, I disagree."

So far, Singapore has only had three prime ministers.

"Singapore's founding PM had an undeniable ability, his successor had guts and initiative." I know Balji is choosing his words, he will talk about the current PM next. "Who we have today is very different. In my personal view, Lee Hsien Loong gives the impression that he is not really decisive. To be fair to him, he is functioning in the towering shadow of his father." He stops, and I get a sense that with a current prime minister, the less said the better.

What about the 4G group of leaders?

"Far more worrisome is the behaviour of the 4G leaders. I have written an assessment of the 4G leaders: I started with a score of 7 out of 10, but reduced it to 6.5. Because I have the experience of working as a journalist when Lee Kuan Yew and Goh Chok Tong were running the show, and this is my personal opinion, but I find this batch of so-called 4G leaders not up to the mark. I don't think they dare make decisions. My mind has been shaped by these two previous leaders, on what to expect from a leader. I find the present leaders to be weak, they do not make difficult and hard decisions, simply because they don't know how. They didn't grow up in that environment. But we have come to a big crisis, possibly the crisis of the century, and we need leaders who can and will make hard decisions. The enemy is invisible, and it mutates. Leaders need to make hard decisions and have the ability to convince the public to follow. In the last two years, I have been very disappointed with these leaders."

He goes back to the fact that he belongs to a lucky generation, his most important years were also the formative years of Singapore. "My definition of a Singaporean was cast and defined during the time of Lee Kuan Yew. Our leaders had guts and they fought for a cause. Even someone like Chee Soon Juan, he never gave up, despite going to jail and being bankrupt. He is always fighting and finally learning to connect with Singaporeans, changing his style. But I don't see that kind of focus and purpose among our 4G leaders, from my personal perspective."

Beyond the leaders, the fabric of Singapore has also changed, people are more informed but their knowledge is sadly without depth. "Perhaps because of how controlled the media is and how materialistic the country has become, people's knowledge of news and current affairs is very low." He stops, wondering how best to be accurate without being unnecessarily harsh. "As a result, they either keep quiet because they have nothing to say, or say things that are totally irrelevant." He manages a smile, "With rare exceptions, there is no real intelligent conversation to be had."

Balji is particularly conscious of one signature trait of the Singapore psyche, which has contributed to a hurried, graceless society: the upgrading mentality. "Over the years, the Singapore government has injected into the minds of its people the need to 'upgrade'. This upgrading mentality and the need to do well (in almost every aspect of life) has led to an essentially 'ugly' people. I was walking on a pathway that allowed basically only two people to walk side by side, and I saw two young men walking towards me and as they approached, they walked 'through' me, as if I didn't exist. I, a man in my 70s, had to make way for them! These are youngsters in their 20s. They were literally breathing down my neck while I was walking past them. It happens on the trains as well, people rushing for seats in the MRT."

He pauses, but I can tell he has a lot more to say about

this. "It has recently been reported that Singapore is the most fatigued place in the world.[16] Singaporeans are caught, everyone owns a home and they are slaves to their mortgage, all are caught in this vicious cycle. Singaporeans work long hours and they have no life outside of work. They have been relentlessly pushed in the pursuit of a good life, where one has to earn his keep, one cannot depend on the government. We have a billion-dollar tuition industry, one of the biggest in the world. I do not know of any other country with a bigger tuition industry than tiny Singapore.

"People are so busy that they have no time to greet each other on the road. This wanting to do well or do better, with no-time-for-anything-else mentality I find ugly and graceless. The *gotong royong* spirit I grew up with is no longer here. I remember with fondness living in the former British naval base: during our festivities, my mother would put goodies on a tray and distribute to our neighbours. I don't see that any more. We are losing our valued social norms, norms that my generation was used to. Those were values we stood for and they are gone."

Balji has a soft spot for the dormitories where the foreign workers stay. He gets worked up when he reads or hears stories of how they are treated, in a sub-human, degrading manner. "I couldn't believe my ears when I found out that foreign workers, even when they have been vaccinated, could not go out of their dorms. They are probably the safest people to be close to, they have all been vaccinated and are tested regularly, but are not allowed out. So, it's like being in jail for these people. They were finally allowed out only because people wrote in to complain, but by and large, no one notices them or says anything to them. Have we become so elitist?

"Where I live, the roads are being repaved, and the workers are there all day, but no one engages them. They can speak English, but no one speaks to them. These people have sons, daughters, wives, families, like you and I. I recently found out that one of them, in his 40s, was hit by bad news. His daughter had committed suicide. I urged him to go home, and he finally did. He has worked in Singapore for 13 years. One of his supervisors said, 'Your daughter died, so what?'"

All these have led to a real sense of alienation for Balji, a sense that he no longer recognises his home. In an article titled "Ageing in an Ageless Singapore", he adds one more dimension to this alienation, the physical environment of Singapore:[17]

> Statistically speaking, I am part of a group whose life journey is likely to end when we are about 84 years old. This is how long a person can expect to live up to in Singapore. For me, that is 11 years to extinction. With Covid breathing down my neck, that time may come earlier and I am not looking forward to the last leg of my journey …
>
> I am, and many of us are, ageing in an ageless Singapore. The city looks younger by the day as roads are dug up, new buildings built, new eateries opened, new condos pushed up.
>
> Some locations look very foreign. Punggol, Woodlands and downtown Singapore look so weird and strange that I just don't want to go there again. The familiar structures are gone, the buildings just look out of place and the interiors are frighteningly confusing that you want to rush out once you are inside.

Familiarity is important as you get older. You don't
want to be shocked out of your senses when you go to
a place that you knew well and now find foreign …

Living in a squeezed Singapore gets to me every day.

He ends off the article thinking about setting up a second
home in another country, where there is more space and the
pace less hectic, but he admits that at 72, that is not going
to be easy as the second home might be even stranger than
Singapore. Yet Kerala, in India, is a real possibility.

"Many people have this misunderstanding of India," he
begins. "Because they think India is essentially what they
see on the BBC or CNA. People are only mindful of the
capitals like Delhi and Bombay. Of course, they are over-
populated, dirty and rapes are reported daily. But if you go
to the South, you'll see a very different India. The standard
of living is high, there are high quality malls, you can get
any branded stuff you want. Most of the places are not
run down, condos and shopping centres may not be of the
standard in Singapore, but they are good enough for many
people, including me.

"If you look at the Covid statistics, Kerala has one of
the highest Covid-19 cases. But if you look at the number
of deaths, it has the lowest. They have very good medical
care, a good medical system because it is run essentially by a
communist state. I had to be admitted to a hospital because
of a small procedure. The attention to each patient was so
good. The doctors don't rush off to attend to other patients
like the ones in Singapore. They have real time for you. I have
a prostate issue, every year when I do my MRI scan, it cost
$400, but the one I did in Singapore was $1,000, more than

double! The service might not have been as good as Khoo Teck Puat Hospital, but it was above average."

On top of and above the cost of living, what matters most are the things one does every day. "The food is very good. And when I say food, I mean the taste, it brings me back to my mother's cooking. But even more important are the conversations I have there. I have made professional friends, journalists working locally and for foreign agencies. And I must say I have great conversations with these people. They have views and they are prepared to articulate and stand by those views. They can talk intelligently about anything under the sun."

Balji alerts me to the book, *Pride, Prejudice and Punditry: The Essential Shashi Tharoor*.[18] Here, the Keralite highlights why the Malayali cultural heritage will always be a magnet for those living and working outside of it. Apart from the fabled coast, gilded by immaculate beaches and leafy lagoons, it is the soul of the land Keralites will always cherish and lay claim to, however far they have drifted away. Tharoor calls it the "Malayali miracle":

A state that has practised openness and tolerance from time immemorial; which has made religious and ethnic diversity a part of its daily life rather than a source of division; which has overcome caste discrimination and class oppression through education, land reform, and political democracy; which has honoured its women and enabled them to lead productive, fulfilling, and empowered lives. Indeed, Kerala's social development indicators are comparable to those of the US, though these have been built on one-seventieth the per capita income of America.

Singapore may be less and less appealing, conversations are not rewarding and the political scene stifling. But what Balji has built personally, his inner circle and network of friends and family will cushion the blow.

Balji is looking forward to spending a few months in Kerala in 2022. "It will be a test," he explains, his voice forceful and somewhat pensive. "I need to know where I can spend more time in, Kerala or Singapore."

Kerala is probably where *home* is, but Singapore is where *family* is. If home is where the heart is, which is home?

NOTES

1   As reported in *The Straits Times*: Jean Iau, "Woman who shouted racist abuse on bus jailed for 4 weeks", *The Straits Times,* 23 June 2021 <https://www.straitstimes.com/singapore/courts-crime/woman-who-shouted-racist-abuse-on-bus-jailed-for-4-weeks>.

2   Malavika Menon, "Police investigating man accused of using racial slur and kicking 55-year-old woman", *The Straits Times*, 10 May 2021 <https://www.straitstimes.com/singapore/police-investigating-man-accused-of-using-racial-slur-and-kicking-55-year-old-woman>.

3   Belmont Lay, "Workers' Party Pritam Singh: Bigoted views need to be called out even if privately held", *Mothership*, 9 June 2021 <https://mothership.sg/2021/06/pritam-singh-racism-interracial-couple/>.

4   Minister of Finance Lawrence Wong's speech delivered at a forum on race and racism in Singapore, organised jointly by the Institute of Policy Studies and the S. Rajaratnam School of International Studies on 25 June 2021. Speech reproduced on CNA website: "In full: Lawrence Wong's speech at the IPS-RSIS forum on race and racism in Singapore" <https://www.channelnewsasia.com/singapore/lawrence-wong-racism-speech-ips-rsis-forum-1941591>.

5   Nigel Chua, Andrew Koay and Jane Zhang, "Mothership Explains: What is CECA & are S'poreans losing out because of it?", *Mothership*, 8 July 2021 <https://mothership.sg/2021/07/what-is-ceca-singapore/>.

6   See note 4.

7   Chew Hui Min, "From babies to casinos: 11 memorable National
    Day Rally speeches", *The Straits Times*, 20 August 2016 <https://www.
    straitstimes.com/singapore/from-babies-to-casinos-10-memorable-
    national-day-rally-speeches>.

8   Martino Tan, "PM Lee mentions 'Pokémon' in his National Day rally
    trailer", *Mothership*, 20 August 2016 <https://mothership.sg/2016/08/
    pm-lee-mentions-pokemon-in-his-national-day-rally-trailer/>.

9   See note 7.

10 PN Balji, "Comment: Race ties in Singapore's workplace – softly, softly
    approach won't work", *Yahoo News*, 1 September 2021 <https://sg.news.
    yahoo.com/comment-race-relations-singapore-soft-approach-075552326.
    html>.

11 See note 10.

12 See note 10.

13 See note 10.

14 Prime Minister Lee Hsien Loong, National Day Rally 2021, speech
    delivered on 29 August 2021 at Mediacorp <https://www.pmo.gov.sg/
    Newsroom/National-Day-Rally-2021-English>.

15 See note 14.

16 Reported by UK bedding manufacturer, Sleepseeker, "Fatigued Cities",
    29 July 2021 <https://www.sleepseeker.co.uk/blog/fatigued-cities>.

17 PN Balji, "Ageing in an Ageless Singapore", *The New Singapore,*
    6 October 2021.

18 Shashi Tharoor, *Pride, Prejudice and Punditry: The Essential Shashi
    Tharoor* (Aleph Book Co, 2021).

Chapter 9

I Want My Life Back

Covid-19 unveils lack of decisive leadership

Leadership

I end this unique year-long journey with Balji by inviting him to my apartment, to reflect on this extraordinary time that we live in. It began with a virus which surfaced in a Chinese seafood and poultry market in December 2019. I was stunned when the Chinese authorities closed off Wuhan by cancelling planes and trains leaving the city, and suspending buses, subways and ferries within it. I asked, how could the Chinese government halt the life of an entire city? Little did I know then that the virus would go on to halt the life of the entire world and change all our lives along the way.

Named after the crown-like spikes on its surface, the virus is now known as Covid, with 19 added to mark the year it emerged. Caused by the severe acute respiratory syndrome coronavirus 2 (SARS-CoV-2) strain, it has infected more than 150 countries. At the time of writing in December 2021, Covid-19 is a worldwide pandemic with more than 270 million cases and five million deaths, making it one of the deadliest in history.

In "living through a global health crisis with no modern-day precedent", as set out succinctly by Nancy Koehn in her article "Real Leaders are Forged in Crisis",[1]

[w]hat governments, corporations, hospitals, schools, and other organizations need now, more than ever, are what the writer David Foster Wallace called "real leaders" – people who "help us overcome the limitations of our own individual laziness and selfishness and weakness and fear and get us to do better, harder things than we can get ourselves to do on our own."

Balji agrees with the sentiments expressed in Koehn's article. "In general, leaders are not born," says Balji, sipping the *kopi c kosong* I had bought for him earlier. "Their ability to help others in dire need is not something they are born with. In a crisis, they rise to the occasion, sometimes even surprising themselves. They are made in tough circumstances, when they are able to help and inspire people in challenging times."

There is evidence that the pandemic has caused a rally-round-the-flag effect in many countries, with government approval ratings rising, as in Italy (at one period +27 percentage points), or causing sitting leaders to vacate their positions (President Trump saw a 6-point plunge in approval). As Covid-19 tears its way through country after country, neighbourhood after neighbourhood, what have we learned about the leadership in Singapore? How do they compare to the rest of the world, all facing an unprecedented, unfolding health calamity?

"Covid-19 has unveiled a lack of decisive leadership," Balji's voice holds a steely edge, suppressing a palpable anger. "And it's not just political leadership. In my personal opinion, what it has exposed, in a deeper way, is a lack of decisive leadership at almost every level of society. Let me turn the tables and ask you, who is a good leader in Singapore now, one that you can trust to lead us out of this?"

Not able to think of a name, I shake my head.

"I have given it a lot of thought. The only person who comes closest is Piyush Gupta, CEO of DBS," Balji pauses, his fingers tapping on the dark wooden table. "He was able to fix structural defects the leaders before him at the bank couldn't. I can't think of anyone else … there is a dearth of good leaders. And this crisis has exposed a lack of leadership in politics especially, because it starts at the top.

"In my book, today's leaders must be bold enough to throw the old playbook away and start afresh with new ideas and thinking. They must have a rebellious streak in them, like LKY and, to a smaller extent, Goh Chok Tong."

I cast my mental net over names I know. Who could be our saviour in this crisis? And why are there no names that are up to par?

"They come untested," Balji begins to explain. "That's the first reason. They have had such a comfortable existence; everything has worked well. Second, no real leader has come forward. Look at the political succession: from Lee Kuan Yew to Goh Chok Tong, and from Goh Chok Tong to Lee Hsien Loong. Now from Lee Hsien Loong to don't-know-who. What does that tell you? In any other country, that would be the norm, but in Singapore, there has been a set pattern, a political precedent. But no more. We were able to set investors' minds at ease, knowing that Singapore was the most politically stable country, no surprises when it came to who would lead the country. Why this predicament now? Because no one wants to join politics, no one with real credentials to lead, that is."

In Balji's mind, a person's decision to join politics cannot be made based on monetary terms alone. And it becomes glaring in a crisis. "Ask yourself, how many people from the private sector have joined politics and risen to prominent ministerial positions of leadership? With a few notable exceptions like Richard Hu and Tan See Leng, no one else. If they can make it big in the private sector, they don't need the public sector. They are invariably richer and still have their privacy, still have their weekends. Most of the people the PAP ends up with are relatively good academicians who see politics as a career, not as a calling to do public good. And in a perverse sort of way, the latter is exposed to be sorely lacking during a crisis like Covid."

I am glad Balji is enjoying the *kopi c kosong*, the brew inducing him into a mood to talk and engage. "What particular aspect of the 3G or 4G leaders do you find most wanting?" From across the table, I can tell I have touched on the nub of the issue.

"The inability to decide," he says, lifting his right hand and lowering it down like a knife. "The indecisiveness is affecting the country," he says with a chop of his hand on the table. "Plus, in the middle of the crisis, they changed the Health Minister from Gan Kim Yong to Ong Ye Kung. Why? Even the best politician needs run-up time to be fully operational. In the face of the biggest health crisis since independence, they changed the person in charge of the Health Ministry. There is no stability in decision-making, it is reactive and a knee-jerk response. If the argument is to give Ong Ye Kung exposure, is this the best time to do it?"

From Lee Kuan Yew to Goh Chok Tong, Singapore was the temple of competence and decisiveness. The island state was known worldwide as a country with a knack for fixing issues; and planning ahead, Singapore style, was so finely tuned, it was seen not as a science but an art. Has time changed this? Has governance become that complex, that difficult?

"Of course, the world has changed and has become more complex," he says, moving his fingers through his thick grey hair. "Especially with Covid and how we all have to decide between the US and China now. Not easy. All the more reason why we need good leadership. It bears repeating, the best leaders emerge out of a crisis. If everything is hunky-dory, anyone can run the country, on auto-pilot."

So, from this crisis, no decent good leaders have emerged?

"Yes, not from the 4G, in my personal opinion. Of course, not all good leaders need to come from a crisis, but it can demonstrate what a potential leader can do," Balji's eyes move, focusing on the view from the apartment. "A good leader needs to listen to people, and hopefully not just like-minded people, but people with opposing views. But my suspicion is they have underestimated Covid, or what Covid can do. They were so confident of handling it until the variant came. And trust me, there will be many more variants."

The present leadership seems to be operating as a group, no one in particular seems to be in charge. Is this good?

"Bad!" Balji almost shouts under his breath. "In a crisis, there should be one person leading, the person the public relates to. When that person shouts, 'Charge!', we charge. You don't shout 'charge' from the back, but from the front. When you don't have that kind of leadership, and instead have three ministers fronting a crisis, and when tough questions are asked, they look at each other. It doesn't give me confidence. In a crisis, responsibility cannot be shared. We all have slightly different views. Someone has to make the final decision and go with it."

Three ministers are put in charge, who is ultimately responsible for ...

"The Prime Minister must make the right decisions," Balji does not let me finish my question. "He decided on Ong Ye Kung. Gan Kim Yong was the Health Minister, why change? Shouldn't the Health Minister be allowed to see this crisis through when he hasn't done anything wrong? Instead, we have a committee. Who makes the decisions? Why safety in numbers? There is a distinct lack of self-confidence. I listen to the interview with the Prime Minister, on the one hand this, on the other hand that ... there is simply no clear direction, from my personal perspective. In a crisis, we need clear directions. I get the feeling they are muddling through because no one dares to make decisions. When there is no confidence, the messaging gets muddled and people get confused."

Balji homes in, with clarity he likens the situation in Singapore to a war, except the enemy here is invisible. "It is a war," his voice dry and crisp to the point of breaking. "Of course, there is the possibility of making the wrong decisions but does it mean you don't act at all? The leader must dare to make clear decisions, charge or retreat. Even if, in the end, it turns out wrong, the leader needs to make the call, otherwise the country is confused and the enemy wins. At times like this, decisions need to be clear, not wishy-washy.

"In my column for *The New Singapore*, I wrote that I want my life back. And many people told me, they also want their lives back. I want to take charge since the leaders don't know how. They tell you, don't leave your house if you don't need to. If you are not vaccinated, the chances of getting the virus are high. Then, even if you have been vaccinated, not once, not twice but three times, if you have (the famous phrase) 'underlying medical conditions', you can still get it. There is always an 'if'. If you do this or if you don't do that, if you want to or if you don't want to … if, if and if. There is always an 'if'. I say, give us the facts!"

Perhaps the leaders don't have the full picture, which explains why their answers are never categorical or clear.

"Then say so," there is a surge in his voice. "They are the highest paid politicians in the world and they can't give me a straight answer."

What exasperates Balji is losing something he now knows we all take for granted – our freedom. In his column for *The New Singapore*, in an article titled "I Want My Life Back", he makes plain his frustration:[2]

Covid fatigue is oppressive. It takes away your freedom, instils fear and makes you irritable. It is made worse when you realise that the promised light at the end of the tunnel keeps coming and vanishing …

As Singaporeans are told to stay indoors as much as possible, I am looking outside my home to bring back some sanity to my life. The political leaders given the responsibility to take the country out of Covid are struggling with their actions and statements. Most times they are reactive, not decisive enough. You can see them backpedalling as the infections and deaths rise. They don't give me much confidence and it is up to us to use their statements as reference matter rather than the gospel truth.

There is no freshness in their words. Phrases like calibrated approach, living with Covid, middle ground approach are repeated ad nauseam. After some time, these words just fly over your head ...

Many were preparing to dine in with more people; but it didn't happen. Frustration crept in and together with this came comments flooding from social media: if more than two people can't dine in, then what about a family of four or more having dinner together at home?

To add salt to fresh wounds was a report that foreign dignitaries in groups of five can drink and eat at restaurants during a Bloomberg conference from November 16 to 19. ...

Inconsistencies like this and the consistently two-digit death rates show that the leadership might be losing its grip on the battle with Covid. What can I do about all these ups and downs, mistakes and bad communications?

I have decided to take my life back.

Country

Prime Minister Lee Hsien Loong has famously said that most Singaporeans say they want to do their own thing, find their own way; but at the first sign of trouble, they turn to the government for quick answers and solutions. The country's first death from Covid-19 was recorded on 21 March 2020. On 20 October 2021, Singapore reported its highest single-day deaths at 18, even when more than 80 per cent of the population had been vaccinated against the virus. It is quite clear now the government does not have ready answers or solutions for everything. Some Singaporeans are terrified, for the first time they feel lost with no one to look up to or guide them. I read on social media a Singaporean saying, "The government should do something, stop the deaths!" Alas, good policies cannot be ordered from a set menu or deaths simply wished away.

In a 2018 opinion piece by Stephanie Siow and Theophilus Kwek,[3] Deputy Prime Minister Tharman Shanmugaratnam was noted to have argued, in an interview with *The Straits Times* earlier that year,[4] that

> … it is essential to "sustain a culture of personal responsibility". Calling this "a crucial social ethic" for Singapore, he stressed that welfare policies should not ultimately act just as a safety net, but galvanise those with "a spirit of aspiration" to do well for themselves.

Yet, in an interview with CNBC, Prime Minister Lee Hsien Loong said he would not apologise for Singapore being a "nanny state":[5]

> "Well, if you asked a Singaporean, on the one hand they'll say, 'Let us do our own things.' On the other hand, when an issue comes out, they'll ask, 'What is the government doing about it?' And they have very high expectations of what the government should be doing, which is right because they've voted for the government and they expect the government to be able to perform. So, we have to keep the balance."

A balance between self-sufficiency and dependency? A tough balancing act, especially when one is used to being dependent.

"It is politically expedient to sustain a dependent electorate," says Balji. "It is useful in an election. The last election was called in the midst of the pandemic. The PAP was confident they could handle it. But when the crisis is protracted, with no end in sight, it becomes a sharp political problem. They have about three years to the next election. At the start of the pandemic, the Singapore government was the poster-boy, praised by almost every country. Now, Singapore is seen differently, and is suddenly on the list of countries *not* to visit. Singapore resorts to using a statistical argument as a defense, that per 100,000, Singapore is still the lowest."

Has Covid-19 shown how dependent Singaporeans are on their government? Singaporeans have voted the PAP in, overwhelmingly over the past decades. They entrusted the PAP with their lives, literally from cradle to grave; and the PAP has, by and large, acted on their behalf. Now, when it becomes clear the leaders cannot make all the decisions for them, they are lost.

"I'll give you an example," Balji shifts himself in the chair. "You live in your parent's house, for 20 or 30 years. One day, your father decides that this is wrong and wants you to leave and stay on your own. What can you do? Do you know how to stand on your own two feet, be independent and self-sufficient? Apartments are expensive, whether you rent or buy. Share with a friend? Not easy, you need to put up with differences between yourselves. We are so dependent on the political leadership that when we need to act on our own, we don't know what to do. So, we get frustrated and you see today, everyone blames the government. The dependence syndrome created over the years is dangerous. And Covid unveiled this dependency starkly."

Would one of the legacies of Covid be a more matured citizenry? Would Covid force flag-waving PAP supporters to be more critical of the government?

"I don't think so," Balji remains stoically realistic. "People I speak to are focused on very minor things, they bitch about small things but they are not looking at the macro picture, like the political leadership … even with the double-digit deaths they are confronted with every day, most in my view would still think this is a good government.

"Why? Because the PAP is all they know, all they trust. They don't have an alternative. It will take a while for the Workers' Party to be a viable alternative. The PAP has a finger in almost every aspect of our lives … from how you grow up to when you retire or get rehired. The way the population has grown, the way we have been brought up, we lap up what the government says, we don't look at what they do critically, or ask if this is the right way or that is the wrong thing to do. When we do question, it's over nitty-gritty stuff.

"For instance, when I wrote a piece on Opposition MP Raeesah Khan, everyone was obsessed that she must step down for lying in Parliament. Few cared to think deeper, or cared to review the parliamentary video showing the lying she committed and how Minister Shanmugam tried to get to the heart of the issue. Fewer thought further about the implications for the Workers' Party, and indeed for the Opposition as a whole. No one wants to think, they just want to react."

In the end, a strong government in Singapore is its biggest strength, but also its biggest weakness and vulnerability, a view expressed by Ravi Menon, the managing director of the Monetary Authority of Singapore, in a lecture in 2021, adding that an over-reliance on one government means it is a society that won't survive a bad one.[6] Now in a digital world, Singapore cannot rely merely on one source of knowledge or wisdom, says Balji in agreement. He echoes Menon's sentiment that Singapore must forge many sources across different segments of people and knowhow. The new world isn't one where the pact is between the leader and the led, but where the leader seeks inputs from as many avenues as possible. A crisis like Covid shows this clearly. The government should be one player among many, yes, an important player and arbiter, but no monopoly of wisdom, it should be open to ideas from all sources.

Menon also recognised that this would "mean more diverse views, more public debate, more messiness, maybe even more confusion before there is consensus or compromise."[7] Balji is energised. "When more people respond, it just means more views, different even opposing views, more lively public debate. But if we can accept this, that not everything needs to be neat and tidy, that differences within a society is a healthy thing, we are taking steps closer to a mature society, closer to an engaged democracy."

Personal

How the Covid-19 virus invades the human body is akin to a hijack, as explained in a *Web*MD article:[8]

A virus infects your body by entering healthy cells. There, the invader makes copies of itself and multiplies throughout your body.

The coronavirus latches its spiky surface proteins to receptors on healthy cells, especially those in your lungs.

Specifically, the viral proteins bust into cells through ACE2 receptors. Once inside, the coronavirus hijacks healthy cells and takes command. Eventually, it kills some of the healthy cells.

But how does the virus affect us emotionally, psychologically – how does it affect our mental health? One needs to catch Covid-19 to feel and know the real physical impact of the virus, but we all feel the mental impact whether we get the virus or not. A recent report in *The Straits Times* shows a spike in family violence and a surge in mental health issues since the circuit breaker kicked in on 7 April 2020.[9] An online survey of 1,000 people in Singapore conducted by market research company Ipsos over the period of 24 April to 4 May 2020 indicated that one in four respondents are not in good mental health.[10]

Balji thinks the Covid-19 pandemic is the single biggest crisis Singapore has faced in a long, long time. If he were to name the key consequence of the pandemic to Singapore and Singaporeans, what would that be?

"I am a man in my 70s, and talking to me, you may not sense it," a quiver disturbs his otherwise calm voice. "There is a fear that has crept in. The fear of catching Covid. When alerted that I was eligible for the first jab, I went to get it. Second jab, I went. And the booster, I went. And I am normally not so obedient. But I want to protect myself. I have two grandchildren, I don't want them to catch Covid; then there is my wife, daughter and son-in-law. All of them are in the back of my mind.

"The key consequence of Covid is realising that life is fragile, we suddenly feel it. Most of us probably didn't think of it before Covid, we were all supermen and women, we would outlast everyone. Also, there are related questions in my head: if I get Covid, will I get equal treatment compared to more powerful people? And can I afford the treatment? Do I even want to be in the hospital? These are things I think about.

"I have never known this fear, and sometimes I don't even know I have the fear. Then it shows up in ways when I least expect it. I go to the *kopi* stall, and a regular guy I know asks me to join him, I hesitate, and even when I do sit down, the entire time I am not comfortable. I talk to everyone, including people like the cleaner. Then he coughs, do I stay or walk away? Questions I never had to ask myself, things I never had to think of or care about before. Now I do."

This is the fear of a man in the most vulnerable age group, a man who knows he can catch Covid anytime and anywhere. And a man at this age who is also a retiree, with no office to go to, no change of scenery from home. If he can't meet his friends, engage in a debate with them, have his regular "talk cock" sessions, how would he cope?

"It boils down to this: to what extent and when do you let go," I can hear the strain in his voice now. "I can't live like a prisoner in my own house. And I can't travel. This affects me quite a lot, I didn't realise it before. I can't go to Kerala, and my friends are all asking me to go. I want to, but there are no flights."

During a pandemic, it's easy to just see the downside – is there an upside for him?

"Something we have all taken for granted, the need to stay healthy," he says, as he puts his index finger to his lips. "And something else, the country can build up the strongest armed forces, but can it protect itself from a virus like this? While we are humbled by this, we now know we need to stay vigilant and be aware that we can be brought to our knees by something like this. Each and every Singaporean needs to know that while we may have a good government, we must also learn to rely on ourselves. Scrutinise and examine everything in front of us. Have a healthy sense of cynicism, don't accept everything just because the government said so."

At 72, Balji keeps his mind engaged all the time. No critical local or foreign news escapes his notice and analysis. On any given issue, not only does he think about it, he believes in thinking critically about it. That, he believes, is the way to grow old gracefully and meaningfully. "I don't want to get dementia," he laughs. "And the only way is to continue to ponder, think, and think hard. And in my own way, still contribute to the society I live in. Now it's Covid, next year it could be something else. What's important is that I am in charge and in control of my own life."

NOTES

1 Nancy Koehn, "Real Leaders are Forged in Crisis", *Harvard Business Review,* Crisis Management, 3 April 2020 <https://hbr.org/2020/04/real-leaders-are-forged-in-crisis>.

2 PN Balji, "I Want My Life Back", *The New Singapore*, 27 October 2021.

3 Stephanie Siow and Theophilus Kwek, "Rethinking Responsibility", Civil Service College, 29 April 2018 <https://www.csc.gov.sg/articles/rethinking-responsibility>.

4 Prime Minister's Office, Singapore, "The Straits Times Interview with DPM Tharman Shanmugaratnam: Social Policies, Spending and Taxes" 11 January 2018 <https://www.pmo.gov.sg/Newsroom/straits-times-interview-dpm-tharman-shanmugaratnam>.

5   Yen Nee Lee and Christine Tan, "Singapore is known as a 'nanny state'
    – and its leader has no apologies", CNBC, 19 October 2017 <https://
    www.cnbc.com/2017/10/19/singapore-prime-minister-lee-on-leading-a-
    nanny-state-jobs-and-succession.html>.

6   Daryl Choo, "For society to mature, Singaporeans shouldn't rely too
    much on Government to solve problems: MAS chief", *Today*, 29
    July 2021 <https://www.todayonline.com/singapore/society-mature-
    singaporeans-shouldnt-rely-too-much-government-solve-problems-mas-
    chief>.

7   See note 6.

8   *Web*MD, "Coronavirus: What Happens When You Get Infected?"
    <https://www.webmd.com/lung/coronavirus-covid-19-affects-body#1>.

9   Jean Iau, "Coronavirus: More cases of family violence during circuit
    breaker; police to proactively help victims", *The Straits Times*, 8
    December 2021 <https://www.straitstimes.com/singapore/courts-crime/
    coronavirus-more-cases-of-family-violence-during-circuit-breaker-police-
    to>.

10 Ipsos Press Release, "1 in 4 Singaporeans say they are not in good mental
    health", 8 May 2020 <https://www.ipsos.com/sites/default/files/ct/
    news/documents/2020-05/ipsos_press_release_singaporeans_mental_
    health_8_may_2020_updated.pdf>.

Chapter 10

Celebrating 73 Years

Relying on the lung power of his grandchildren.

Date: 30 December 2021 – Balji's 73rd birthday. The Covid restrictions are still in place, so the birthday party I invited myself to at 27 Clover Way is an intimate affair. I had texted him earlier:

You prefer Indian or Japanese whisky?

Indian.

Good. I thought you would say both.

Momentary lapse. Both!

I know Balji likes Amrut, the single malt whisky from India. Most whisky lovers like the blended Japanese Hibiki. I decide to buy both, but as it turns out, both are out of stock at my usual liquor store. So I buy Glenfiddich, the reserve single malt. The label says it comes from one of the oldest family-owned single malt distilleries in the world, so it should be good.

The party starts between 6.30 and 7pm. As I arrive, a tall young man walks out of 27 Clover Way, he turns and waves. My god, Arrian! He must have shot up five inches since I last saw him two months ago. "Let me walk you to the door, I locked it on the way out," he says. His fingers tap out the password numbers on the lock keypad by the door. The sound of the party flows out as it opens.

The small party has started, with family and relatives; I am the only "outsider". Deepa catches my eye, "I want to show you something." She walks me to the kitchen, suppressing a giggle. "Look, Arrian has set up a bar!" The 13-year-old has decided that the alcoholic gifts his grandpa receives are too messy and uncoordinated. On the kitchen counter, he has written in bold, block letters, "WELCOME TO THE BAR". Alcohol of all types are neatly assembled below the words. Perfect – I put my bottle prominently in front of the rest.

The birthday boy is talking to his brother, Sivaji. I settle myself on a sofa opposite Balji as Deepa brings me a glass of wine. His brother was a football coach in Myanmar for almost a decade, but Covid and the military coup brought that to a screeching halt.

"You still get news from Myanmar?" I had met him when I was running a TV channel there two years ago.

Sivaji's face knots, "Yes, I get sad news from my former colleagues."

International, local and family news mix like rojak; adults, teenagers and kids test, enter, stay or withdraw from each other's universe. This is the world Balji has grown into, every other day is a discovery of what new tricks his grandsons are up to while negotiating his own world of news, routines and new ventures.

"I will go to Kerala for only a month and a half, February and March, I need to be back end-March," Balji says, as he and his friend are preparing a pitch for a major event in Singapore in 2022. "I need to be around."

The womenfolk bring out the food from the kitchen, and the smell of mutton *biryani* reminds me that I had skipped lunch. As I sip my wine, I see Arrian making his way to his grandpa. Sitting next to him, he looks more like a son than a grandson. I can't hear their conversation, so I watch the body language and their faces. Looking at Arrian's legs, he will be taller than Balji in no time. But it is also clear that this grandfather is someone he will always look up to, no matter how tall he grows. From time to time, Arrian puts his hand on his grandpa's shoulder. When Balji goes back to Kerala, Uma will join him. Arrian and Roman will miss their grandparents, probably more than their grandparents will miss them. And that alone is a remarkable familial gem.

In addition to the mutton *biryani*, there is a spicy fish dish and chicken prepared in a mixed masala sauce. Deepa asks if I want a second glass of wine. "By the way, I am not sure if my father has told you, we are moving in with my parents in the middle of January," Deepa smiles as she sees the look of surprise on my face. "They are aging, and this is the only way we know how to look after them. Of course, we have asked them to stay with us, but they don't want to move out of their comfort zone and I think it's a lot easier for us to move in here than for them to move to our apartment. So yes, I'll be leaving my Sky Pool behind."

With a fresh glass of wine, I walk over to the dining table and join Balji. My mind flashes back, to the time he told me how his heart broke when he was not able to see Deepa off to school in the morning, and the promise he made to himself not to be late again; Deepa looking at his Filofax, pages and pages of "spend time with Deepa"; his published letter to Arrian … This daughter has grown up. There is a silly saying about sons and daughters, but somehow it doesn't seem so silly now – "A son is a son till he takes him a wife; a daughter is a daughter all her life."

"You must try the rice," Balji moves the red-hot rice dish towards me. "And the *biryani*, the white sauce goes with it, especially if you find it's too spicy."

"Thank you," I skipped lunch for this, so I move in to eat. "When does Divya arrive?"

He had mentioned his second daughter would be coming from Toronto in January 2022; it will be a rare occasion, the whole family together again.

"First week of January," he looks up as he replies. "She will self-quarantine here."

After dinner, Arrian prepares a game for everyone, where we need to have our mobile phones to participate. There is then a commotion as Sri, Deepa's husband, directs the party towards the dining table again. Before us is a two-tier birthday cake with two rows of pink striped candles. A newspaper, rolled up to reveal *The Birthday Chronicle*, is placed carefully between the candles. This, I suspect, is the handiwork of Sri, Deepa and Arrian.

Balji enlists his two grandsons to help him blow out the candles as the birthday song is sung.

And so the birthday evening dissolves into games and drinks, the games led by the youngsters and the drinks by the not-so-young. No one asked Balji what his birthday wish was before he blew out the candles. My guess – there was no birthday wish. The birthday man lives in the present, and the present is damn good, 73 years on.

*****

Post-birthday: Friday, 31 December 2021. Balji posts on Facebook a birthday card drawn by his younger grandson, eight-year-old Roman. He thanks everyone for their birthday wishes and adds, "This was the best gift." The card is a pencil-drawn sketch, of two people in a Mercedes-Benz. The boy is depicting Balji and Uma, because one of the figures has longer hair. Both obediently have their seat belts on. Inscribed on the card:

HAPPY BIRTHDAY, to the world's best GRANDPA!
You mean the world to me. I love you so very much.

There is no manual for good parenting or good grandparenting, no hard and fast rules. Each family navigates within its own parameters of personalities, characters and experiences, and learn and do better. Yet who the adults are and how they hold themselves up as examples are important. As we move further and further away from traditional families to modern ones, it is heartening that some families, like Balji's, hold on to some traditional values. Moving back to be with her parents, Deepa collapses the roles of daughter, wife and mother into one, a fusion of tradition and modernity.

In the end, Balji's Singapore story is a story of love, sometimes hard and tough love. His love for gathering, assessing, creating and presenting news and information made him the journalist and editor his staff remember. An intense love-hate relationship with Singapore that propels him to be a commentator and critic. It's Singapore first, not PAP or Opposition. And family – even at his busiest, it was and always has been, family first. Both his daughters feel and know it. Now his grandchildren get the taste of it, the kind of love that knows when to hold on tight, and when to let go.

This last part is for his wife, Uma. The shy young girl from Kerala, India, whose faith in marriage and family brought her to Singapore. For this story, true love is not about Romeo and Juliet who died together. It's grandma and grandpa who will grow old together.

Annex

After the 2020 General Election, Balji felt strongly that politics in Singapore had to change. "It is not just that politics must move away from the old paradigm, but so must the academic, political commentator, businessman and, most important of all, the Singaporean," he stressed.

We decided to start *The New Singapore*, a Facebook page where Balji could express his thoughts. "It is a small contribution from a small man living in a small country who has lots of time to eavesdrop, observe and read."

Balji talked to all kinds of people: "The uncles who go to the coffee shop at regular hours to just chat, foreign workers who toil away under the hot sun, young people who have an opinion on everything under the sun, my grandsons who are signalling to me that a silent revolution is taking place in our homes and any person who I come across during my daily walkabouts."

These walkabouts resulted in many popular articles. I have selected some of the best articles published by *The New Singapore* to be reproduced here. These were hot topics with lay Singaporeans over the last two years and continue to be relevant today. The final article "Lawrence Wong Must Move Away from the Same-Same Approach" was written specifically for this book.

A New Singapore
17 July 2020

If GE2020 had shown something clearly and starkly, it is about how Singapore politics must change. It is not just that politics must move away from the old paradigm, but so must the academic, political commentator, businessman and, most important of all, the Singaporean.

Talking about this with my comrade-in-arms, founding editor of Channel NewsAsia, Woon Tai Ho, we concluded that I should kickstart a series of articles on *The New Singapore* that GE 2020 has unleashed on the country. During the august period of my life I have no grand ambition to do a New Deal, a series of programmes initiated by former US President Franklin Roosevelt to get his country out of the Great Depression.

It is a small contribution from a small man living in a small country who has lots of time to eavesdrop, observe and read. Since joining the gig economy 12 years ago (long before the phrase became fashionable), I have been trying to read the mood of a nation that is buffeted by the small man's angst, big people's power play and the middle class' struggle to find a life.

I talk to all kinds of people. The uncles who go to the coffeeshop at regular hours to just chat, foreign workers who toil away under the hot sun, young people who have an opinion on everything under the sun, my grandsons who are signalling to me that a silent revolution is taking place in our homes and any person who I come across during my daily walkabouts.

Some conversations stick forever. At a Bishan coffeeshop, I asked a 60-year-old waiter a simple question: *Apa macam?*

(How are you?) He asked me if he could sit down and launched into an emotional monologue about his life. His wife is sick, his son suffers from a terminal illness and he gets about $1,000 a month. How to manage like this?

He wanted to unburden everything on me. I listened, nodded and nearly teared. What else could I have done? I could have given him a gift but that was not going to solve his problems. Every time I go there, he receives me warmly and brings my beer, and I don't take the change. His wide toothless grin tells me he appreciates my gesture.

Once I was on my evening walk at Bishan Park where I met an Indian foreign worker who was a few steps in front. I caught up with him and asked: *Eppidi?* (How are you?) He spoke about his life, when he came to Singapore, his family back home and concluded: you know something, no Singaporean has spent time talking to me like you have done.

My grandson, Arrian (12), is developing a voice of his own. He has a view on everything and he expresses it strongly and clearly. I asked him what he thought of Trump. He shot back: Dumb. I was dumbstruck for a moment. Before I could recover and respond, he had vanished. Today's young is like that; they have drawn their own caricatures of people, countries and events, and express them without fear.

There is a young journalist, angry, restless, free-spirited and will chase a story till he lands it. He is never happy with his work, always pushing for the next big thing. But the organisation he works for doesn't know how to satisfy him. There is nobody there to counsel and cajole him. He sends me cryptic messages reflecting his present state of mind. I am quite sure he won't last in that organisation.

This election result brought back memories of these and many others who have come into my life since 2008. Some have disappeared, others have remained. They are the silent forces who came to life to tell us that Singapore is changing. Politicians who are serious about the next election, you all better start talking and listening to them and many others like them. They are going to change Singapore in ways unimaginable.

Will *The Straits Times* Change?

24 July 2020

The grand old dame of Singapore journalism is 175 years old. *The Straits Times* is older than the PAP and independent Singapore. The newspaper is an institution that should be celebrated, respected and revered. Yet we hardly see any signs of joy. The chronicle has had a chequered history that campaigned against the PAP when British editors ruled. Mr Lee Kuan Yew's party won that election in 1959 and the editors, fearing that they will be arrested, ran away to KL to produce the paper. Sometime later, they returned on bended knees and did Lee's bidding.

Lee learned two things from this episode: editors can be easily cowed and their bosses are mainly interested in making money from their newspaper business. From that episode, Singapore's press law was born. The Newspaper and Printing Presses Act, which made the licensing of newspapers a central feature of media control, came into force in 1974. The Act has been amended a number of times; one of the changes led to foreign publications being forced to publish government replies in full to correct reports that it considered inaccurate. If they refused, their advertisements would be blacked out. Over time, publications like *The Economist* and *The Washington Post* surrendered to the will of the Singapore state with even the owner of the *Post*, Katharine Graham, flying in to make peace with Lee.

Over and above the press laws, the government used other measures to tame *The Straits Times*. When the editors tried to push back, they were moved out. The signal to those who took over was loud and clear: toe the line or get shipped to the paper's Siberia. The current set of young editors know which side of the bread is buttered and produce a newspaper which is plastered with speeches of ministers and government announcements.

Nearly 90 per cent of the news comes from the government and very little effort is used to produce news about Singaporeans and the lives they lead. Their aspirations and their struggles living in a small city that depends on the vagaries of the policies of their neighbours and the world at large are hardly published. The reporters' go-to place is Facebook. And the readers' the *South China Morning Post*. The journalists pick up news from FB and go to the government for a response. *The Straits Times* then uses the response to angle the story. The result: initiative disappears and the paper looks like a government mouthpiece.

GE2020 has shown the declining influence of ST and the growing popularity of social media. The swing against the PAP started after Nomination Day when the ruling party used bully tactics to frighten voters, especially the young ones. A Blackbox survey found that slightly over half of Gen Z voters went to social media for election news. Only 10 per cent got it from newspapers.

I expect this trend to grow as ST is unlikely to change the way it covers news, especially government-related news, over the next few years. What makes it worse is the government's control of media. I am not just talking of the press laws but also control in other forms. ST's executive chairman is a former government minister, its CEO is from the military, and government ministers from the PM downwards hold lunch meetings to try and convince journalists of the need for some unpopular policies.

When journalists write about these policies, those meetings play in the background. It is very difficult to shake them off. The result is reports that come across to many as government press releases.

Occasionally, a journalist comes out into the open about his/her frustration. A former political reporter with *The Straits Times* said in a FB post recently that she gets upset when people say opposition candidates are not good. This was part of the media machinery that helped enhance this image, she wrote. Good opposition candidates were always there, but voters hardly heard about them, the journalist lamented.

The reporter gave an example of how censorship works. She wrote about a respected opposition candidate in 1997. "I tried my best to give him and his team fair coverage. Once I even managed to get full page coverage for his party. "Boy was there hell to pay the next day," she wrote.

Nearly every journalist who worked in ST has such stories to tell. Some get into the public domain, others the news people take to their graves.

I don't see the government relaxing its hold on ST in the near future. But the editors can try and push the boundaries. Businessman Ho Kwon Ping asked the paper to "tell truth to power" in its anniversary supplement. Former editor-in-chief Peter Lim told the editors rather pointedly to understand the limits and have the guts to draw the line, too.

Guts. That is a rare commodity in our newsrooms.

And the public seems to have given up on the paper. They have begun to desert the paper for other sources of information online. They must have come to the conclusion that the marketplace will dictate the fate of ST as its circulation and advertising revenue continue to tumble.

The paper can avoid collapse if the biggest stakeholder in the business, the government, concludes that there is no light at the end of the tunnel. Or if the editor comes to the realisation, as Peter Lim has said, that as leader of the newsroom he has to display some guts and draw a hard line on the sand.

I don't see either scenario playing out in my lifetime.

What Is Ho Ching Up To?

2 August 2020

What a wasted opportunity. Instead of having a meaningful and dispassionate discussion on the Leader of the Opposition concept, we are seeing verbal diarrhoea being spewed on the merits and demerits of whether Pritam Singh should have made it public that he was donating part of his increased allowance to charity.

With Ho Ching entering the fray, the discussion just went downhill. Her arrow was aimed, obliquely perhaps, at Singh, although she didn't mention his name in her FB post. She seemed to be upset that many others give to charity, but then don't publicise it. And the "most handsome genius" Calvin Cheng was also there in the trenches calling Singh's action political theatre.

The CEO of Temasek's indirect attack attracted a lot of attention because she is no ordinary woman. She is a corporate leader and the PM's wife. Which of the two hats was she wearing? Or was she writing as a citizen, or as the conscience of Singapore society?

Ho Ching is so into social media that she can share or write multiple posts in a day. Some are about inane topics like food and animals, others are about what PAP leaders are doing. We can take comfort from the fact that she is not as bad as Donald Trump, who goes berserk in attacking his rivals by throwing smoke bombs and using intemperate language.

But what does her husband, the PM, think of his wife's posts? Has he advised her against doing it? Or is he the modern husband who doesn't want to interfere in his wife's affairs? Whatever his views, her actions cannot be wished away as she is the most important woman in Singapore. And what she says on Facebook will be sliced and diced to unimaginable conclusions. It will lead to splitting an already polarised society.

OK, she has kind of apologised but water has already flowed under the bridge and the wounds are not going to be healed soon.

The Leader of the Opposition is worthy of a deep scrutiny and debate because it can shape the future of Opposition politics. Many feel that it is a scheme to draw Singh and his comrades into a trap to be slaughtered.

The PM mentioned it at least three times that he was looking forward to seeing alternative proposals from the Workers' Party. For that to happen, Singh and company will need all — and I emphasise ALL — the help from civil servants, who should not second-guess or hold back from giving information.

The PAP holds the cards in this game. It has many more people, much more experience and much more information. It can turn out to be an unfair affair. The burden is on the ruling establishment to show it is sincere. If there are gaps in WP's arguments, reveal them but do not gloat over the Opposition's mistakes. And stop the inquisition-like approach, which some have tended to display.

As for Singh, he has to present watertight ideas and, if proven wrong, show sincerity and contrition. This is like a Liverpool-Leeds United football match. Liverpool is always the favourite to win against underdog Leeds. But look at the way Reds manager Jurgen Klopp treats his rivals with compassion and empathy.

If both PAP and WP play the game with Singapore uppermost in their minds, then we are on to something.

Weary Nation, Wounded Nation

7 August 2020

In a couple of days, Singapore will mark its 55th birthday. With the jobless rate going up, families being separated by shuttered borders, Covid-19 and dengue plucking away lives and movements outside your homes being restricted, what is there is to celebrate?

What we are seeing is a weary nation. Beneath that surface, an angry and wounded nation is surfacing. It has been simmering for a while and would have remained under wraps if not for GE2020, which fast-tracked the exposure.

I didn't realise the intensity of the feeling until I received text messages from two friends, one 60 and the other in his early 50s. The political leadership was the target of their ire. One said: "… And they (political leaders) still think they are God's gift to Singapore … Safe to say it is one of the weakest Cabinets in Singapore's history. As a Singaporean, I have never felt more disappointed with our leadership than in this GE."

Phew. The pent-up emotions just flowed. What makes this outburst worrisome is that he used to be very considerate and balanced in his views.

At about the same time, I got a younger man's flurry of messages. He went on and on, and just couldn't stop. After launching a tirade against *The Straits Times*, he said: "I seriously question the efficiency of the multiple officer-holders in a typical PAP Cabinet line-up. Won't this mean more red tape? Failed to see the logic behind this."

Singapore is reaching a tired phase of its growth with the establishment keeping to its old playbook and the citizens wanting a society that is more than super structures like

Jewel, the upcoming Tuas port and the new Marina Bay downtown.

My sense is that Singaporeans are looking for a soulful country that will treat EVERYBODY equally and with the same respect. Former minister Yaacob Ibrahim confirmed in a video interview with Walid Jumblatt Abdullah of NTU that the mood against PAP changed after Nomination Day. If that is so, then the PAP has to realise that all the effects of good initiatives – like the four budgets costing nearly $100 billion – can be easily forgotten by just a couple of hasty and ill-conceived actions like the attack on WP candidate Raeesah Khan and the way the ruling party left new candidate Ivan Lim to fight his own battle with social media over complaints of his behaviour against his military mates.

We are seeing the early signs of a new Singapore emerging where citizens are not going to accept lying down the old paternalistic approach to governance. Fairness is becoming the name of the game of engagement.

Here is my wish list for a new Singapore on its 55th birthday.

RELOOK past policies which are sitting like an albatross round the government's neck. First on the list is a policy that disappears and reappears at regular intervals. High ministerial salaries have remained a contentious issue. The first official recognition of how it is dividing society came after the 2011 elections, when Lee Hsien Loong cut salaries substantially and got some ministers to resign after his party took a beating.

That was the boldest political move by Lee since he became PM in 2004. Two main reasons were given when the salary plan was debated in Parliament: to make sure that politicians and civil servants will not allow their palms to be greased and to get talented people into government. Anti-corruption is already embedded in the Singaporean's DNA and the CPIB's no-nonsense attitude to graft can take care of that. As for talent, it is debatable if high salaries have got talented people into government. The struggle to get such people, especially since 2011, shows that the establishment's record has, at best, been patchy. Each time the citizen perceives an office-holder unworthy of top pay, the salary debate goes into high gear. Finally, the government cannot wish away the argument that government service is public service and money should not be used as a lure to get people to serve.

Another contentious issue is the government's control of mainstream media. It goes back to the Newspaper and Printing Presses Act 1974. A newspaper company has to get a licence to publish news. This kind of control does not fit Singapore's image as a modern society. The government control has become very deep-seated so that even senior civil servants have no qualms about calling editors to angle stories that will make the government look good. My sense is that editors have given up fighting their cause.

This can only mean that mainstream media is losing its relevance and more people are moving to social media for their news fix. Singapore needs a more vibrant media and one way to achieve that is to free the press from the shackles of government.

The PM is on the last leg of his leadership. If he can unwind these two policies, he will be remembered for a long time.

It Is All About PM's Personal And Political Legacy
4 September 2020

People of my vintage would sit rooted in front of the TV set waiting for Lee Kuan Yew to give his National Day Rally speech. He hardly disappointed, except when he raised issues that shocked and angered the nation. In his 1983 speech, he poked into our bedrooms to dictate that graduate mothers should be given tax breaks and priority for their children's school admission. He was on the side of nature and against nurture in the eugenics debate, arguing that highly-educated women produced smarter kids.

The howls of protests from Singaporeans were epitomised in a letter in ST accusing the PAP of behaving like Nazi era storm troopers. The uproar from Singaporeans showed up in the votes they cast in the GE a year later with a swing of 12.9 per cent of votes against the ruling party. In the end, the graduate mums policy and Lee's eugenics experiment were abandoned.

Lee was famous for his combative and forceful style, leaving very little to the imagination of his audience. Still, we sat there watching him speak year after year, marvelling at the way he thundered (most times) and cajoled (sometimes). Goh Chok Tong was very different: he was gentle, didn't speak off the cuff and had a teleprompter to help him keep to his message. A rally speech that created a stir was his last one as PM in 2003. Many of us were surprised when he brought up an allegedly scandalous incident about his successor, Lee Hsien Loong. He quoted from a book, *Governance in Singapore* by Ross Worthington, which said Lee Jr had slapped Minister S Dhanabalan.

Many in the audience were shocked and felt the incident had actually happened. Others asked why Goh had to bring this up at a time when Lee Jr was going to take over from him. That mystery continues till today.

Now to Lee Hsien Loong. As usual, I was there in front of the TV set on Wednesday, listening intently as he admitted to some government missteps in fighting the Covid-19 menace. But the tone changed once he switched gears and turned to politics. He shed his statesman-like image and went on a highly partisan approach with the PM mentioning his party's name countless times.

GE 2020, which saw his party lose a second GRC and a significant swing away from the ruling party, seemed to weigh on him. He accused the Opposition WP and those who voted for it as free-riders because they knew PAP would still run the country and thus they can have the cake and eat it. This is not really a new phenomenon in Singapore's electoral history. Once, Opposition leader Chiam See Tong engineered a by-election strategy by getting his compatriots to contest the right number of seats to leave PAP in power on Nomination Day. The Opposition thus blunted the fear that voting for the Opposition in large numbers won't lead to a freak election result with PAP losing power.

The disappointment in the PM's words was clear. This is likely to be his last term as PM and he was leaving office with his personal and political legacy under a dark cloud. Under his leadership, the party lost Aljunied GRC in 2011 and now Sengkang GRC. Electoral history has shown that once the Opposition makes inroads, it is difficult for PAP to change electoral outcomes. JB Jeyaretnam did that by breaking the PAP monopoly by winning the single seat of Anson in 1981;

there was no looking back after that and an Opposition presence in Parliament has remained since. It is easy to make that same connection to the GRC losses.

But GRCs carry a bigger risk as a PAP defeat in these so-called super constituencies means more than one PAP member being sent home packing. Under Lee's watch, some ministerial heavyweights like George Yeo had to leave office. It is this backdrop that must have made Lee launch his attack on WP and those who voted for it.

But evidence from those who followed the polls suggests that there was something else that led to PAP's poor showing. Former minister Yaacob Ibrahim said in an interview with NTU lecturer Walid Jumblatt Abdullah that the PAP was headed for a big victory until Nomination Day. But the mood began to change after voters saw how the PAP reacted to Raeesah Khan's alleged comments on race and religion. PAP was quick off the block and asked for a response from WP. Pritam Singh handled his candidate's situation with aplomb, leaving many to connect the political dots and link the final image to the PAP's behaviour.

The electorate is maturing; they want a strong and credible Opposition in Parliament. Whether inside the House or outside, the elected politicians are being watched. I watched the debate between the PM and the Leader of the Opposition and that between Jamus Lim, PAP MPs and Tharman Shanmugaratnam closely. They can only be good for the political maturing of a nation.

Not Time To Parti Yet … Let's Wait For The Real Verdict On The Liew Mun Leong Affair

13 September 2020

It was a moment of serendipity with a number of stars lining up in the Singapore sky to form a constellation that must have made many of us proud. The timing could not have been more perfect. The country was moving towards a them-and-us polarisation with the debate over politics, the disadvantaged, foreigners and race popping up again. We needed something to unify the country. Indonesian helper Parti Liyani's success in the Appeals Court, which acquitted her of all five charges of theft, brought a number of forces together to show that the justice system is not really broken, although some aspects of it were exposed to the administration's embarrassment.

The coming together of a noble lawyer, an NGO fighting against the odds, a judge who spoke truth to power, the helper who wanted to prove her innocence and a social media which, on most occasions, wanted to keep the story on the boil.

In the end, we saw a well-connected corporate chieftain being forced to step down as chairman of the Changi Airport Group and from other top posts. Liew Mun Leong had a powerful team to craft a polished image of a tycoon who became a darling of the media and the establishment. In the process, the companies that he helmed benefitted.

But the PR playbook he nurtured shrewdly could not save him from one of the most spectacular downfalls in recent corporate history. He forgot the basics of PR: in a crisis, you must not remain silent and must act with speed. If you don't, a news vacuum will be created with others rushing in to fill the space.

Liew was savvy enough to know the power of media. When he was CEO of Capitaland, he made it a point to have his corporate communications team on the floor where his office was. He told one of his senior managers: I need to meet you and your people very often and need you all within hearing distance. Finance and HR were also on his floor, but "I don't need to meet them often."

His PR team arranged lunch meetings with the bigwigs of media regularly and fed stories to them to boost his image and indirectly the image of the companies he headed. But all that media cultivation did not rescue him as Liew faced the biggest crisis of his corporate life. Even the wording of his press statement announcing his resignations became a social media controversy. He said he was bringing forward his "retirement". Even *The Straits Times* chose not to use that word, but instead picked the phrase "steps down".

Liyani was a brave woman. Her lawyer, Anil Balchandani, took up her case free of charge and a group of activists fighting for her rights, the Humanitarian Organisation for Migration Economics, helped to find a shelter for her and, not to forget, the Home's moral support. Justice Chan Seng Onn questioned the two important pillars of the Singapore justice system: the police and the court. Both did not come out looking good. The police took five weeks after Liew made an official report to start its investigation and the lower court appeared to have not paid enough attention to the gaps in the Prosecution's case.

Home and Law Minister K Shanmugam has said his officers will find out what went wrong. This is the elephant in the room. What the Minister needs to establish is what went wrong in the "chain of events". Was it because the lower court and the police were not thorough enough due to Liew's high stature and his connections?

This goes to the heart of the debate in Singapore about whether elitism has seeped into the system and exposed a decay in our moral system. If this issue is not addressed to satisfaction, then the work of the helper, lawyer, migrant activists and the judge will be wasted.

The time has not come to Parti. Not yet.

Post-Covid, Singapore Politics Must Change
29 September 2021

The Singapore government's political honeymoon is being chipped away as the establishment struggles and stumbles to tame the Covid monster. It is nearly two years since the public has been rattled by restrictions, relaxations and more restrictions.

And the complaints, even from people who used to jump to defend the ruling government, are getting louder by the day. One was very upset with the hospital crunch he experienced when he went to seek treatment in a hospital. "I was there for five days. I saw hospital beds in the corridor, doctors and nurses scrambling to treat patients … This is a scene I would associate with a Third World country, not a modern nation like Singapore."

My personal Covid moment happened when I read the news on Sept 22 that hospital ward visits will not be allowed for a month. I follow Covid news reports religiously. Yet, there was nothing that prepared me, and I presume many others, for this shock to the system. A friend talked about his trauma when his 90-year-old mother, who has a history of strokes, was hospitalised recently. He could not be with her because of the restrictions. He found a way to communicate with her via the laptop he got a nurse to pass to her. "… she was incoherent and she couldn't recognise me. She appeared very frail," he said.

As the new restrictions kicked in on Monday and as light in the tunnel gets dimmer by the day, the time has come for Singaporeans to ask what the country will be like once the virus is tamed. Instead of getting frustrated and angry over how the government is faltering in its response, our time will be better spent hitting the pause button and focusing on the political changes the country must introduce as the 4G leadership tries to establish its mark on how the country is run.

Our immediate future depends on this group and it will be a good opportunity to think about how their playbook must change.

Covid has exposed the yo-yo way the leadership tried to achieve a landing with as few mishaps as possible. Which phase of the game plan are we in? So many terms like Dorscon Orange, circuit breaker, heightened alert and transition phase have been thrown up that just serve to confuse the people. For the PR people, these are words they like to spin out of nowhere. But for the ordinary people struggling to keep their lives decent and sane, they mean nothing.

As I look at the press conferences and Facebook posts of the ministers put in charge of taking us out of the pandemic, I am aghast at how out of touch they are. They allowed the Ministry of Health to declare those with mild symptoms to recover at home. "These patients must be able to self-isolate in a room, preferably with an attached bathroom," it said. Now, somebody missed the ground reality that not all flats have attached bathrooms. In the grand scheme of things, this may not be such a big thing but it shows how little our civil servants and politicians know about life in Singapore.

Such slip-ups go to the heart of how the PAP chooses its leaders. The emphasis is on those who have solid degrees from the best universities. Then there are the military generals who come to the rescue when the numbers are not enough for a general election. They are all intelligent but not smart to make decisions during the worst crises like Covid that the country is facing now.

These leaders need to listen intently to what citizens and critics are saying. Listening is one thing, acting is another. If they had done both, the dormitory calamity would unlikely have happened.

We need leaders who must have a streak of rebelliousness in them. Leaders who are brave enough to move out of their comfort zone and come out with unthinkable solutions for a country that is moving on listlessly.

These people must not be ring-fenced by laws and older leaders. They must be thrown into the lion's den and told to fight their own battles. Let them fall, get up and fight again. Some will fall by the wayside, some will survive and some will just give up. Out of this baptism of fire will emerge a bunch of politicians who should be able to take Singapore to a new future.

I Want My Life Back

27 October 2021

Covid fatigue is oppressive. It takes away your freedom, instils fear and makes you irritable. It is made worse when you realise that the promised light at the end of the tunnel keeps coming and vanishing. Many were hoping to get back a semblance of their life last Wednesday but then came the announcement that the flickering light of freedom can be seen only on Nov 21, or earlier, if hospitalisations stabilise.

I am not going to wait until Nov 21 to take my life back. I will be going for my weekend *idly* breakfast at Suriya restaurant, a nondescript corner of Little India. It is not just the food I miss; the service is excellent, not to mention the smell of Chennai that attacks your nostrils.

There is my neighbourhood coffee shop, Jakopi, where my friends meet daily for non-stop chats on politics (what else?), children and grandchildren, and the occasional debate on a nasty neighbour who complains about the noise we make.

The characters who work there are your everyday aunties who know each one of us by our names or by nicknames they have given us. They work non-stop with hardly any time to rest; having some spare time to just sit down is a luxury. They come from homes that people like me are hardly familiar with. It is the place you go to if you want a dipstick understanding of a country that, if you scratch the surface, exposes its hidden Third World status.

There is the occasional drive to my former neighbourhood in Naval Base in Sembawang to brood over the good times lost. A drive past the black and white bungalows on roads displaying names like Montreal, Wellington and Canberra is a must. There are pockets in the area that have hardly changed. Occasionally, a police car comes by to see if I am up to some mischief as US Navy personnel live in these spacious bungalows. Going to Sembawang Park to walk on the jetty to see how close JB is and watching the Marine Police looking for illegal immigrants trying to sneak into Singapore shows how close yet how far we are from neighbour Malaysia.

On my drive back home, a pit stop at the narrow and short stretch called Sembawang Strip is a must as it brings back memories of the British Navy people engaging in rowdy and raucous banter.

As Singaporeans are told to stay indoors as much as possible, I am looking outside my home to bring back some sanity to my life. The political leaders given the responsibility to take the country out of Covid are struggling with their actions and statements. Most times they are reactive, not decisive enough. You can see them backpedalling as the infections and deaths rise. They don't give me much confidence and it is up to us to use their statements as reference matter rather than gospel truth.

There is no freshness in their words. Phrases like calibrated approach, living with Covid, middle ground approach are repeated ad nauseam. After some time, these words just fly over your head. The biggest disappointment came last Wednesday when many people's expectations of having a freer life were burst when the government announced that the restrictions will continue for another four weeks.

Many were preparing for dining in with more people, but it didn't happen. Frustration crept in and together with this came comments flooding from social media: if more than two people can't dine in, then what about a family of four or more having dinner together at home?

To add salt to the fresh wounds was a report that foreign dignitaries in groups of five can drink and eat at restaurants during a Bloomberg conference from Nov 16 to 19. The information appeared in a note from EDB Chairman Beh Swan Gin to forum delegates. Why did Beh think that this won't get out, especially when a foreign media group is the organiser of the forum?

Inconsistencies like this and the consistently two-digit death rates show that the leadership might be losing its grip on the battle with Covid. What can I do about all these ups and downs, mistakes and bad communications?

I have decided to take my life back.

In Death, Schooling Leaves Behind A Gift For Fathers
24 November 2021

During a chance encounter with former Foreign Minister George Yeo, a proud Colin Schooling said of his Olympic champion son: "This is my gift to Singapore." Before you jump to any conclusion that Colin was being impudent, Yeo dashed that thought when he recounted to *TODAY* in 2016: "There was no conceit ..."

And if you go away thinking that the gift was the historic Olympic gold medal feat by his son, Joseph Schooling, in Rio in 2016, then you are doing a great injustice to the 73-year-old who passed away on Nov 18 after he lost his fight against cancer.

The gift was for all fathers, many of whom struggle daily to balance work, leisure and family.

Colin is an extraordinary father who did everything – yes, everything – to make sure his only child won big at the Rio Olympics.

Colin's passion – call it obsession, if you want – came to light in the way he prepared meticulously and doggedly to crack Singapore's toughest nut, Mindef, to get NS deferment for his son. I interviewed him for *The Independent Singapore* soon after that victory five years ago. The father's commitment, tenacity and attention to detail – nearly every detail of his son's training regime, exploits in the pool and discipline – shone through in his presentation to Mindef.

He said: "Every swim competition from 2000 (the day he started to race) at five years old till 2009 (the time he left for the US to study and train at age 13) was documented and monitored ... Joseph's successes and present status were not a flash-in-the-pan story but a result of many years of hard work.

"Nearly every local and international event Joseph took part in was documented. May (his wife) and I would have our worksheets ready to monitor his reaction times off the block, split times, stroke counts and strike rates. We did this so that we could be constructive in our opinions and advice to our son. We could not just rely on his coaches totally because they were busy with others under their charge."

Not to forget the swimming aids like tailor-made goggles and a drag chute attached to the waist to build the swimmer's strength and endurance through resistance. Nothing was left to chance. Everything was planned to precision and recorded.

Armed with all the details, the parents presented their voluminous report to Mindef. It was difficult for the Ministry to say no and thus Joseph became the first youth to get deferment.

The parents did not stop there. They wanted to learn all aspects of swimming, especially the technical aspects. So they built an extensive swim library at home, took the swimming association officials' credential tests, attended many courses and lectures conducted by experts, served as honorary treasurers in the swimming association for two years. "We played hosts to many visiting Olympic swim teams from the US, Canada, Australia, Switzerland, France, Italy ... "

Colin knew that money would be an issue as the government's track record in this area was nothing to crow about. The parents decided to go it alone to pay for their son's education and training in the US. They sold their property in Australia and ended part of their insurance endowment plan to finance their son's journey to become a champ.

You can see what an exceptional dad Colin was. As I reread the interview I did with him, the question I asked myself again and again was this: how many such dads, including myself, are there here? Zilch, I would dare to say.

If we dads can do even 10 per cent of what Colin had done for his son, we will go some way to being good parents. As the Singapore family faces the pushes and pulls of modern life, Colin can stand as a beacon on how to manoeuvre the potential minefields.

Colin has left behind a gift for all of us. Let us unwrap this gift and savour his tireless effort as a father to bring glory to his son and Singapore. Colin Isaac Schooling is the true son of Singapore and a true father of the Singapore family.

Forgotten Parents
1 December 2021

My grandson has entered teen hood. I asked him how he felt about this new stage in his life. "Nothing, lah. It is all the same. But I am expecting an increase in my allowance," he said with a cheeky smile and looked to see the reaction on his mother's face. She knows her son too well; her face was expressionless.

Arrian is firm about one thing. "I want to be an aeronautical engineer," he told a friend of mine. I asked him a pointed question: do you have a girlfriend? His instant answer floored me: "Girlfriend will suck money out of you." I have no idea where he got this idea from. But I let his statement go, hoping to raise it at another time.

When my children were growing up, such questions were never asked. Today, parenting has become very different and complex. With both parents working and with children exposed to tech gadgets and peer influence, we are very watchful about what they see, talk about and do.

Grandparents have a different role to play in this new world, that of adjunct parents. The role is a complementary one where we watch carefully how the parents interact with the children and keep to the same methods and values. For one, we don't use baby language to talk to them. Like their parents, we talk to them like we would to adults. Words have to be in full sentences and they need not be simple ones. The last thing we want is to send conflicting signals to the young ones.

The results are seen in how Arrian and his younger brother speak. Yes, they speak like adults.

Communication between parents and grandparents is important. The other day, Arrian's dad told me about an incident the boy faced in the train. He banged accidentally into a lady, who he said reacted rudely and loudly to him. He said he apologised to her. But she went on scolding him. "Arrian was very upset," said the dad.

I decided to bring up the incident with Arrian a few days later. I wanted to inject a sense of perspective and asked him if he had experienced similar incidents. No, he said. "This is what life is about. The majority are good people, only a small minority are like the lady on the train. In life we must take a balanced approach."

He listened intently, but said nothing. I knew he had got the message.

My wife and I are not intrusive. We move in only when we are told to do so or when Arrian and his brother, 8, are with us. We try and get involved in their activities, listen to them intently and ask very short and pointed questions.

The one missing piece in the modern family, as far as I have seen, is the growing role of grandparents. It is not about spoiling the grandchildren by stuffing them with unhealthy food and buying them expensive toys. These are things they couldn't do for their own children because they were busy with their work. Their role is about being there for the parents, stepping in when we are needed to help. And, not to forget, taking the grandchildren out on purposeful activities which they are fond of.

Roman, the younger boy, is very interested in art. So I took him to see the mural paintings in Chinatown. I wanted to show him some of the paintings on my phone before we went. He said: "No need, then there is no surprise." Hmmm.

He enjoyed being up close and personal with the paintings and posed for pictures. Roman loves to draw and I am a fan of his artwork. One day, I asked him: "When do you decide to take up your brush and paint? Do your paintings reflect your mood, like do you do it when you are angry?"

He thought for a while, then said: "Yes, especially when I am angry with my brother."

"Can you show me some of those paintings?"

"I have thrown them away."

I am glad to see him express his emotions this way.

Last weekend was Grandparents' Day. There was hardly any mention of it in the media or by our politicians. Contrast that with the big bang way Mother's Day, for example, is celebrated.

It tells a lot about how our society is ignoring the role of grandparents. Sad.

Balji with Roman, 2016.

Lawrence Wong Must Move Away From The Same-Same Approach

It is a quality that you can't help but admire. The Singapore government has this ability to get its politicians, civil servants, grassroots people, and even businessmen and women, to put up a show of unity when there is a need to close ranks and sing just one tune. Dissent, especially open dissent, is frowned upon.

When the PM announced that Lawrence Wong had been picked as the leader of the team that will rule the country, the impression foisted upon the public was that everything was hunky-dory. The truth is something else.

Lurking in the announcement are cracks in the narrative that this political succession is not going according to script. First, it was the decision to get the zen-like wise old man, Khaw Boon Wan, to see who in the Cabinet wanted who to be the leader. It was clear that the PM had wanted somebody who was generally respected to get the succession going. Khaw was a senior minister and chairman of the ruling PAP. It was a departure from the previous two processes that saw a small group representing the next generation leaders pick their leader.

Second, the decision by the PM and his two senior deputies to take themselves out of the decision-making process was not just rare but also strange. Why couldn't he have followed the past practice of getting their own kind to pick their leader, like they did in the past two successions? Even if there was disagreement among the 4G leaders, would it not have been the responsibility of the PM to step in to act?

And Khaw's involvement in the choice saw an "overwhelming" majority of the Cabinet, including the 4G leaders, choose Lawrence Wong as the leader. But four of the 19 were not for Wong. That shows some kind of open dissent against Wong.

A rock-solid political succession is one of Singapore's plus points. But this time round, it has been too slow and a little disruptive. The man originally anointed to become the leader, Heng Swee Keat, appeared clueless and confused when he spoke about his East Coast plan after his nomination for the last election in 2020 was announced. Then he threw in the towel after the PM said he was not stepping aside just yet as he felt obliged to hand over power after Covid-19 has been tamed. Heng felt his runway had been cut short. He was already 60.

Now that Wong has been picked as the heir apparent, the question to ask is this: What kind of leader will he be? Does he have the smarts to ride all the rough challenges the new world is throwing up and take the country to a new era?

His biggest test came when he was made co-chair of the Covid task force. With the backing of the entire government machinery and the support of an obedient public, Wong and his team succeeded in managing Covid.

Bigger tests are on the horizon. Singaporeans will want to know how Wong is going to resolve the sticky problem of foreigners working here. Intellectually, the argument for outsiders to add to the pool is something that cannot be disputed. But emotionally, it is a very divisive issue as many remember how the government went overboard in bringing in foreigners without any consideration for the feelings of Singaporeans. What angered many was the fact that the government, known for its strategic thinking and scenario planning, lifted the floodgates for foreigners without thinking through the after-effects, like the housing and transport crunch, that their entry would cause.

Trust Distrust, until then a foreign word in Singapore, began to take root. Twelve years later, the political leadership has yet to shake off this albatross round its neck. One of Wong's priorities is to retry and restore the displaced trust.

Trust will again be needed as racial polarisation crops up now and then with more and more Singaporeans not being coy to talk about it. There are issues like Chinese privilege, racial divide and the divide between Chinese Singaporeans and Chinese immigrants and Indian Singaporeans and those who come from India. The frustrations Indian Singaporeans have shown against those from India can boil over in no time. Again, it falls on Wong's shoulders to carry the ground not just with subtlety but with some hard talk on the realities he sees as the PM of the country.

Foreign relations, especially with China, are simmering. Singapore has played a delicate and difficult balancing game between the US and China as the two powers jostle for economic supremacy. Singaporeans have yet to hear what his views are on this potential time bomb.

Wong's plate is overflowing. In trying to clear the issues one by one, the one quality he needs is to be his own man. He cannot use the old political playbook and talk about Singapore's limited talent pool, the dangers of allowing the racial and foreigner divide to boil over, and the need for Singapore to manage the China-US economic and security rivalry behind closed doors.

Wong needs an independent streak to manage these fissures. More than that, he needs a rebellious mindset that Lee Kuan Yew showed in the early days.

Acknowledgements

I will remember 2021 for many things, but the most rewarding memory is writing this book, and getting to know Balji, the man and his family, chapter by chapter. Today, when I take the train to Bishan, it's almost like "going home", that walk from the station to 27 Clover Way has been etched in my mind.

The book began with a close friend suggesting the title *On Clover Way*, since Balji and his family have lived in the same house for more than 40 years. It took form when the institution of family recurred again and again as writing progressed. The girth developed when we explored retirement and Balji's "second act", and gained heft when he assessed the transitional crisis of the ruling party and its handling of the Covid-19 pandemic.

When the book was finally completed at the end of the year, it had gone beyond Clover Way, and we knew it was a book about transition – of an individual, a family and a country. *Transition* became the natural title of Balji's story. So, the first person I need to acknowledge is the man himself, for trusting me to share his life story, and extending the trust for a whole year. We almost exhausted all available venues in Clover Way for breakfast and lunch. His patience and willingness to dig deep within himself gave me the words for this book. I have observed and learned many things from Balji, and one aspect that bears repeating is his respect for his fellow human beings, old or young, female or male, poor or rich, dark, brown, yellow or fair. There is no qualification in his accord of pure respect for another individual.

Uma, I want to acknowledge and thank specially. She is the other lead in this story, even though she doesn't appear as much as the main lead. An unforced presence and the author of her own fortune, she takes what life offers then turns it on its head. A non-threatening, low-key, self-made woman. It was my pleasure getting to know the lady.

Deepa, Sri and Divya cheer-led the book, always available, always positive. Interviews and exchanges with them were absolute delights. But the biggest hoot I had was my session with Arrian and Roman, the grandchildren. Their spontaneity was infectious and their approach to family reminded me of how children look up to adults, reinforcing the importance of adults' attitudes. The cheer they brought underlined what Balji reminded Arrian of in his letter (see Chapter 4), that "children bring tremendous joy to your life" and "life will become more balanced and meaningful". Writing this book highlighted many aspects of family missing in my own life, but it also made me see what I do have and must treasure.

Balji's primary focus is family, and has famously said he has very few friends. Yet, the many I have spoken to were very happy to make time and share their experiences and thoughts about him. On the work front, Irene Hoe was a gold mine: for this book, she spared many evenings texting me, and an entire afternoon, bringing along Zainah, who in turn brought along sheets of messages documenting their unusual boss-staff exchanges.

MD Saleem is an unusual man, the segment on him shines light on the special relationships Balji has with individuals who struggle at the margins of society. Balji has two daughters and also a few "sons" he shelters under his wings.

The changing relationship with Peter Lim, from colleague to good friend, speaks volumes of the type of professional Balji is. Peter Lim's view of and approach towards women, and what he did for his mother was a piercing moment in the book.

Agatha Koh, thank you for providing a different perspective, William Chua for that eternal smile. And we cannot forget Gangsta Sista and Mama-san – our Monday mornings would have been very different without them.

I want to thank Melvin Neo and Ethel Tan at Marshall Cavendish International (Asia) for believing in the PN Balji story. An author couldn't have asked for a warmer reception to his manuscript. And Anita Teo-Russell, thank you for being such a cool, sensible and practical editor.

Finally, ShuQi for being such a good friend to Balji and I, and Wee Siang for his moral support in the course of the journey.

About the Author

Woon Tai Ho is a writer and media veteran. He wrote his first book, *To Paint a Smile*, in 2008. The genre-defying book weaved political, economic and social events into the art and philosophy of Singapore's renowned artist, Tan Swie Hian. Since then, he has been a prolific writer. Tai Ho wrote his first novel, *Riot Green*, in 2013. He has written two books on artist Lim Tze Peng; the second, *Soul of Ink*, has been translated into Chinese. He is also involved in George Yeo's *Musings*, a three-series book to be launched over 2022 and 2023.

In media, he is best known for starting the Asian-wide news channel, Channel NewsAsia in 1999. In the course of more than two decades, he launched news and entertainment channels across Asia, including MiTV and Channel K in Myanmar.